"Modern people often view the fear of God with disdainful suspicion, but Michael Reeves shows us that godly fear is really nothing other than love for God as God. Reeves also helps us to see that the greatest factor in promoting the fear of God is knowing his grace in Christ. As John Bunyan said, 'There is nothing in heaven or earth that can so awe the heart as the grace of God.' This wonderful book not only teaches but sings, leading us to 'rejoice with trembling' (Ps. 2:11)."

Joel R. Beeke, President and Professor of Systematic Theology and Homiletics, Puritan Reformed Theological Seminary

"We used to sing a hymn that said, 'O how I fear Thee, living God! With deepest, tenderest fears.' No longer. But the hymn's first lines remind us of what we are missing: 'My God, how wonderful Thou art, Thy majesty, how bright.' Only those who find God to be 'wonderful' and his majesty 'bright' experience the 'tenderest' fear. So we have a problem; but thankfully help is at hand in *Rejoice and Tremble*. Like an elder brother, Michael Reeves guides us into a fresh understanding of the fear of the Lord. On the way, he introduces us to some of his friends—masters in the school of discipleship—who have walked the path before us. Join him on the journey. You will soon discover why 'the LORD takes pleasure in those who fear him' (Ps. 147:11)."

Sinclair B. Ferguson, Chancellor's Professor of Systematic Theology, Reformed Theological Seminary

"The fear of the Lord is the beginning of wisdom, the Bible says, and reading this book will make you wise—wise to who God is and what God requires of us by way of loving, responsive discipleship. Packed full of historical nuggets, *Rejoice and Tremble* deserves to be widely read. 'Walking in the fear of the Lord' is language that has largely disappeared from the contemporary church. The result is the insipid quality of a great deal of current Christianity. Recapturing the sense of God's incomprehensible greatness and holiness is the needed antidote this book provides. An absolute gem of a book."

Derek W. H. Thomas, Senior Minister, First Presbyterian Church, Columbia, South Carolina; Chancellor's Professor of Systematic and Pastoral Theology, Reformed Theological Seminary

"Ours is a day of great fears—fear of financial collapse, fear of terrorist attacks, fear of climatic disasters, fear of a deadly pandemic—all kinds of fears, except the most important of all: the reverential fear of God. How needed then is this marvelous study of a much-neglected theme, one that is central to the Scriptures and vital to human flourishing."

Michael A. G. Haykin, Chair and Professor of Church History, The Southern Baptist Theological Seminary

"Michael Reeves has given us something we badly need and likely haven't realized—a fresh encounter with the thrilling fear of the Lord. This book will bring renewed devotion and delight. Having read it, I can't wait to read it again!"

Sam Allberry, apologist; Associate Pastor, Immanuel Church, Nashville, Tennessee

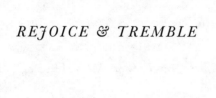

REJOICE & TREMBLE

Union

A book series edited by Michael Reeves

Rejoice and Tremble: The Surprising Good News of the Fear of the Lord, Michael Reeves (2021)

What Does It Mean to Fear the Lord?, Michael Reeves (2021)

REJOICE
&
TREMBLE

*The Surprising Good News of
the Fear of the Lord*

MICHAEL REEVES

WHEATON, ILLINOIS

Library of Congress Cataloging-in-Publication Data

Names: Reeves, Michael (Michael Richard Ewert), author.
Title: Rejoice and tremble : the surprising good news of the fear of the Lord / Michael Reeves.
Description: Wheaton, Illinois : Crossway, 2021. | Series: Union | Includes bibliographical references and index.
Identifiers: LCCN 2020019610 (print) | LCCN 2020019611 (ebook) | ISBN 9781433565328 (hardcover) | ISBN 9781433565335 (pdf) | ISBN 9781433565342 (mobi) | ISBN 9781433565359 (epub)
Subjects: LCSH: God (Christianity)—Worship and love. | Fear of God—Christianity.
Classification: LCC BV4817 .R34 2021 (print) | LCC BV4817 (ebook) | DDC 231/.6—dc23
LC record available at https://lccn.loc.gov/2020019610
LC ebook record available at https://lccn.loc.gov/2020019611

Crossway is a publishing ministry of Good News Publishers.

VP		31	30	29	28	27	26	25	24	23	22	21
15	14	13	12	11	10	9	8	7	6	5	4	3

For Rob and John, my dear friends

———

In a perfect Friendship this Appreciative Love is, I think, often so great and so firmly based that each member of the circle feels, in his secret heart, humbled before all the rest. Sometimes he wonders what he is doing there among his betters. He is lucky beyond desert to be in such company. Especially when the whole group is together, each bringing out all that is best, wisest, or funniest in all the others. Those are the golden sessions; when four or five of us after a hard day's walking have come to our inn; when our slippers are on, our feet spread out towards the blaze and our drinks at our elbows; when the whole world, and something beyond the world, opens itself to our minds as we talk; and no one has any claim on or any responsibility for another, but all are free-men and equals as if we had first met an hour ago, while at the same time an Affection mellowed by the years enfolds us. Life—natural life—has no better gift to give. Who could have deserved it?

C. S. LEWIS, *The Four Loves*

Contents

Series Preface

OUR INNER CONVICTIONS AND VALUES shape our lives and our ministries. And at Union—the cooperative ministries of Union School of Theology, Union Publishing, Union Research, and Union Mission (visit www.theolo.gy)—we long to grow and support men and women who will delight in God, grow in Christ, serve the church, and bless the world. This Union series of books is an attempt to express and share those values.

They are values that flow from the beauty and grace of God. The living God is so glorious and kind, he cannot be known without being adored. Those who truly know him will love him, and without that heartfelt delight in God, we are nothing but hollow hypocrites. That adoration of God necessarily works itself out in a desire to grow in Christlikeness. It also fuels a love for Christ's precious bride, the church, and a desire humbly to serve—rather than use—her. And, lastly, loving God brings us to share his concerns, especially to see his life-giving glory fill the earth.

Each exploration of a subject in the Union series will appear in two versions: a full volume and a concise one. The idea is that church leaders can read the full treatment, such as this one, and so delve into each topic while making the more accessible concise version widely available to their congregations.

My hope and prayer is that these books will bless you and your church as you develop a deeper delight in God that overflows in joyful integrity, humility, Christlikeness, love for the church, and a passion to make disciples of all nations.

Michael Reeves
SERIES EDITOR

1

Do Not Be Afraid!

BOO!

It's one of the first words we enjoy. As children, we loved to leap out on our friends and shout it. But at the same time, we were scared of the dark and the monsters under the bed. We were both fascinated *and* repelled by our fears. And not much changes when we grow up: adults love scary movies and thrills that bring us face-to-face with our worst fears. But we also brood and agonize over all the dark and dreadful things that could happen to us: how we could lose our lives, health, or loved ones; how we might fail or be rejected. Fear is probably the strongest human emotion. But it is one that baffles us.

To Fear or Not to Fear?

When we come to the Bible, the picture seems equally confusing: is fear a good thing or bad? Is fear something to embrace or to flee? Many times Scripture clearly views fear as a bad thing from which Christ has come to rescue us. The apostle John writes: "There is no fear in love, but perfect love casts out fear. For fear has to do with punishment, and whoever fears has not been perfected in love"

(1 John 4:18). Zechariah, the father of John the Baptist, prophesied that Jesus's salvation would mean

> that we, being delivered from the hand of our enemies,
> might serve him *without fear*,
> in holiness and righteousness before him all our days.
> (Luke 1:74–75)

The author of Hebrews agrees, arguing that Christ came specifically to "deliver all those who *through fear* of death were subject to lifelong slavery" (Heb. 2:15). Indeed, the most frequent command in Scripture is "Do not be afraid!"

Yet, again and again in Scripture we are called to fear. Perhaps even more strangely, we are called to fear *God*. The verse that quickly comes to mind is Proverbs 9:10:

> The fear of the LORD is the beginning of wisdom,
> and the knowledge of the Holy One is insight.

But while that is the best known, it is far from alone. At the start of the book of Proverbs we read,

> The fear of the LORD is the beginning of knowledge;
> fools despise wisdom and instruction. (1:7)

David prays,

> Teach me your way, O LORD,
> that I may walk in your truth;
> unite my heart to fear your name. (Ps. 86:11)

Isaiah tells us that "the fear of the LORD is Zion's treasure" (Isa. 33:6). Job's faithfulness is summed up when he is described as "a blameless and upright man, who fears God" (Job 1:8). And this is not merely an Old Testament state of affairs that the New Testament rises above. In the Magnificat, Mary says that

[the Lord's] mercy is for those who fear him from
generation to generation. (Luke 1:50)

Jesus describes the unrighteous judge as one "who neither feared God nor respected man" (Luke 18:2). Paul writes, "Since we have these promises, beloved, let us cleanse ourselves from every defilement of body and spirit, bringing holiness to completion in the fear of God" (2 Cor. 7:1); and again, "Bondservants, obey in everything those who are your earthly masters, not by way of eye-service, as people-pleasers, but with sincerity of heart, fearing the Lord" (Col. 3:22). Clearly, the New Testament agrees with the "Preacher" when he concludes Ecclesiastes: "The end of the matter; all has been heard. Fear God and keep his commandments, for this is the whole duty of man" (Eccles. 12:13).

In fact, the fear of God is so important a theme in Scripture that Professor John Murray wrote simply, "The fear of God is the soul of godliness."[1] The seventeenth-century Puritan John Owen likewise argued that in Scripture, "the fear of the LORD" means "the whole worship of God, moral and instituted, all the obedience which we owe unto him."[2] And Martin Luther taught in his Small Catechism that the fulfillment of the law means "we are to fear, love, and trust God above all things."[3] Walking his people through the Ten Commandments, Luther wrote that a right understanding of each meant knowing "we are to fear and love God."

---

1   John Murray, *Principles of Conduct: Aspects of Biblical Ethics* (London: Tyndale, 1957), 229.
2   John Owen, *Temptation and Sin*, vol. 6 of *The Works of John Owen*, ed. William H. Goold (repr., Edinburgh: Banner of Truth, 1967), 382.
3   Martin Luther, *The Small Catechism, 1529: The Annotated Luther Study Edition* (Minneapolis: Fortress, 2017), 217.

All of which can leave us rather confused. On the one hand, we are told that Christ frees us from fear; on the other, we are told we ought to fear—and fear God, no less. It can leave us discouraged and wishing that "the fear of God" were not so prominent an idea in Scripture. We have quite enough fears without adding more, thank you very much. And fearing God just feels so negative, it doesn't seem to square with the God of love and grace we meet in the gospel. Why would any God worth loving *want* to be feared?

It is all made worse by the impression that *fear* and *love* are two different languages preferred by two different Christian camps—perhaps two different theologies. The one camp speaks of love and grace and never of fearing God. And the other camp seems angered by this and emphasizes how afraid of God we should be. The fear of God is like cold water on the Christian's love for God. We get the impression that the fear of God must be the gloomy theological equivalent of eating your greens: something the theological health nuts binge on while everyone else enjoys tastier fare.

My aim now is to cut through this discouraging confusion. I want you to rejoice in this strange paradox that the gospel both frees us from fear and gives us fear. It frees us from our crippling fears, giving us instead a most delightful, happy, and wonderful fear. And I want to clear up that often off-putting phrase "the fear of God," to show through the Bible that for Christians it really does *not* mean being afraid of God.

Indeed, Scripture will have many hefty surprises in store for us as it describes the fear of God that is the beginning of wisdom. It is not what we would expect. Take just one example for now. In Isaiah 11:1–3 we are given a beautiful description of the Messiah, filled with the Spirit:

> There shall come forth a shoot from the stump of Jesse,
> and a branch from his roots shall bear fruit.

And the Spirit of the LORD shall rest upon him,
> the Spirit of wisdom and understanding,
> the Spirit of counsel and might,
> the Spirit of knowledge and the fear of the LORD.
And his delight shall be in the fear of the LORD.

Those last two statements should make us question what this fear of the Lord is. Here we see that the fear of the Lord is not something the Messiah wishes to be without. Even he, in his sinless holiness and perfection, has the fear of the Lord—but he is not reluctant about it. It is not that he loves God and has joy in God but finds (unfortunately) that to fulfill all righteousness he also must fear God. Quite the opposite: the Spirit who rests on him is the Spirit of the fear of the Lord, and his *delight* is in the fear of the Lord. It forces us to ask, what is this fear, that it can be Christ's very delight? It cannot be a negative, gloomy duty.

Today's Culture of Fear

But before we dive into the good news the Bible has about our fears and the fear of God, it is worth noticing how anxious our culture has become. Seeing where our society now is can help us understand why we have a problem with fear—and why the fear of God is just the tonic we need.

These days, it seems, everyone is talking about a culture of fear. From Twitter to television, we fret about global terrorism, extreme weather, pandemics, and political turmoil. In political campaigns and elections, we routinely see fear rhetoric used by politicians who recognize that fear drives voting patterns. And in our digitalized world, the speed at which information and news are disseminated means that we are flooded with more causes of worry than ever. Fears that once we would never have shared cross the world in seconds and are globally pooled.

Our private, daily routines are filled with still more sources of anxiety. Take our diet, for example. If you choose the full-fat version on the menu, you're heading for a heart attack. Yet we're regularly confronted with the latest discovery that the low-calorie alternative is actually carcinogenic or harmful in some other way. And so a low-grade fear starts with breakfast. Or think of the paranoia surrounding parenting today. The valid but usually overblown fear of the kidnapper lurking online or outside every school has helped fuel the rise of helicopter parenting and children more and more fenced in to keep them safe. Small surprise, then, that universities are now expected to provide previously unheard-of "safe spaces" to protect or quarantine students. Children have grown up so protected that they are not expected to be able to cope with opposing viewpoints or criticism. It is just one indicator that they are considered more fragile than students were a generation ago.

However, it is wrong to single out the pejoratively named Generation Snowflake: as a whole, we are an increasingly anxious and uncertain culture. Anyone in management knows about the staggering proliferation of bureaucratic red tape around health and safety. Yet it has not made us feel safer. If anything, we triple-check our locks even more obsessively. The certain safety we long for evades us, leaving us feeling vulnerable, like victims at the slim mercy of everyone and everything else.

And therein is an extraordinary paradox, for we live more safely than ever before. From seatbelts and airbags in our cars to the removal of lead paint and asbestos from our homes, our safety is guarded more than our shorter-lived ancestors could have imagined. We have antibiotics to protect us from infections that in other centuries would have been all too easily fatal. But rather than rejoicing, we worry we're becoming immune and so heading into a post-antibiotic health apocalypse. Though we are more prosperous and secure, though we have more safety than almost any other society in history, safety has become the holy grail of our culture. And like *the* Holy Grail, it is something we can never quite reach. Protected like never before, we are skittish and panicky like never before.

How can this be? When we are so cushioned as a society, why is the culture of fear so strong today? Professor Frank Furedi writes: "Why Americans fear more when they have far less to fear than in other moments in the past is a question that puzzles numerous scholars. One argument used to explain this 'paradox of a safe society' is that prosperity encourages people to become more risk and loss averse."[4]

There may be something to this. We certainly are free to want more, have the chance to own more, and often feel the right to enjoy more. And the more you want something, the more you fear its loss. When your culture is hedonistic, your religion therapeutic, and your goal a feeling of personal well-being, fear will be the ever-present headache. For all that, though, Furedi argues that the "paradox of a safe society" actually has deeper roots. It is, he maintains, *moral confusion in society* that has led to an inability to deal with fear, a rise in anxiety, and so an increase in the number of protective fences erected around us.

Furedi's argument is especially interesting given that he is an ardent humanist, not a Christian. It is insightful and surely right of him to look for deep roots to our culture of anxiety. I suggest, though, that he has not dug deep enough. Furedi's argument is that moral confusion

---

4 Frank Furedi, *How Fear Works: Culture of Fear in the Twenty-First Century* (London: Bloomsbury, 2018), 22.

has left our society anxious. However, moral confusion itself is a consequence of a *prior* loss: the fear of God. It is God who provides the logic and matrix of morality: when he is no longer feared, moral confusion must follow. In other words, moral confusion is not the root of our anxiety: our moral confusion today and our general state of heightened anxiety are *both* the fallout of a cultural loss of God as the proper object of human fear.[5] That fear of God (as I hope to show) was a happy and healthy fear that shaped and controlled our other fears, thus reining in anxiety.

With society having lost God as the proper object of healthy fear, our culture is necessarily becoming ever more neurotic, ever more anxious about the unknown—indeed, ever more anxious about anything and everything. Without a kind and fatherly God's providential care, we are left utterly uncertain about the shifting sands of both morality and reality. In ousting God from our culture, other concerns—from personal health to the health of the planet—have assumed a divine ultimacy in our minds. Good things have become cruel and pitiless idols. And thus we feel helplessly fragile. No longer anchored, society fills with free-floating anxieties. (Where fear is a response to something specific, anxiety is more of a general condition, like something in the atmosphere. Anxiety can therefore latch on to anything and morph effortlessly in a moment: one minute we are concerned about knife crime, the next about climate change.)

---

5 I do not mean to imply that Western "Christian" culture was once necessarily filled with more regenerate believers who had a right fear of God. Rather, a broader cultural acknowledgment— even a sort of fear—of God provided the framework for a more commonly assumed respect for moral order. Moreover, the church's influence on the culture was greater, and a right, believing fear of God provided the heart and soul of a wider appreciation that we live in this world under the just and holy eye of God.

The Fearful Legacy of Atheism

The suggestion that our loss of the fear of God is the root cause of our culture's anxiety is a real blow to atheism. For atheism promised exactly the opposite. Atheism sold the idea that if you liberate people from belief in God, that will liberate them from fear. This is how Bertrand Russell argued the case in 1927 in his famous address *Why I Am Not a Christian*:

> Religion is based, I think, primarily and mainly upon fear. It is partly the terror of the unknown, and partly, as I have said, the wish to feel that you have a kind of elder brother who will stand by you in all your troubles and disputes. Fear is the basis of the whole thing—fear of the mysterious, fear of defeat, fear of death. Fear is the parent of cruelty, and therefore it is no wonder if cruelty and religion has gone hand-in-hand. It is because fear is at the basis of those two things. In this world we can now begin a little to understand things, and a little to master them by help of science, which has forced its way step by step against the Christian religion, against the Churches, and against the opposition of all the old precepts. Science can help us to get over this craven fear in which mankind has lived for so many generations. Science can teach us, and I think our own hearts can teach us, no longer to look round for imaginary supports, no longer to invent allies in the sky, but rather to look to our own efforts here below to make this world a fit place to live in, instead of the sort of place that the churches in all these centuries have made it.[6]

---

6 Bertrand Russell, *Why I Am Not a Christian* (London: George Allen & Unwin, 1957), 22.

While Russell tragically misunderstands what it means for the Christian to fear God, one struggles not to laugh at how wildly inaccurate his prophecy has turned out to be. For, nearly a century after he said those words, it should be clear to even the most vision-impaired mole that throwing off the fear of God has not made our society happier and less fretful. Quite the opposite—a point acknowledged by the staunchly atheistic professor Frank Furedi, who has become perhaps the global expert on our modern culture of fear.

Of course, it was not only Bertrand Russell who argued that more self-dependence and less fear of God would help us. The whole premise of the Enlightenment was that the advance of our knowledge would dispel our problems and our superstitious fears. This confidence in human reason was classically depicted in the frontispiece to Christian Wolff's marvelously ambitious *Reasonable Thoughts about God, the World, the Human Soul, and All Things in General* (1720). The engraving shows the happy sun of knowledge lighting up the gloomy old world of faith, driving away the shadows and the darkness of fear and superstition. A cheery thought indeed for the eighteenth century; but, again, quite the opposite has happened. Today, while we all (sort of) love our smartphones and our GPSs, we acknowledge that the advance of knowledge is a mixed blessing. For it is all too apparent now that new technologies have consequences we cannot foresee. When, for example, you first bought a smartphone, you had no idea of its toll on your social behavior or your sleep patterns. When first you used social media, you saw some potential bonuses but had no concept of how it would feed your fear of missing out. More knowledge does not necessarily mean less fear; it often means more.

Perhaps the greatest irony, though, is that the free-floating anxiety that fills our "enlightened" and godless society is really nothing more than the same primitive superstition we thought knowledge would eradicate. In 1866 Charles Kingsley delivered a lecture at the Royal Institution in London entitled "Superstition."[7] In that lecture he defined superstition as that fear of the unknown which is not guided by reason. Which is precisely what we see all around us. It is not obvious to us that our fears are actually superstitious, for, said Kingsley, we always endeavor to make our superstitions look reasonable. To prove his point, Kingsley gave the example of the fifteenth-century textbook on witchcraft the *Malleus Maleficarum*. Seeking to make a science out of witch-finding, this text fueled a fear-filled superstitious urge to find witches by giving that urge an apparently scientific basis. According to the *Malleus Maleficarum*, you could not question the reality of witches in our midst—it was a reasonable and scientifically verifiable concern. But superstition it was, Kingsley argued. And despite great strides in knowledge, such unquestioned, fear-inducing superstition remained in his day. Mere advance in knowledge and technology does not eliminate fear.

So, what does our culture do with all its anxiety? Given its essentially secular self-identity, our society will not turn to God. The only possible solution, then, must be for us to sort it out ourselves. Thus Western, post-Enlightenment society has medicalized fear. Fear has become an elusive disease to be medicated. (I do not mean to imply here that use of drugs to curb anxiety is wrong—only that they are a palliative, at times an important one, and not an ultimate solution.)[8] Yet that attempt to eradicate fear as we would eradicate

---

7 Charles Kingsley, "Superstition: A Lecture Delivered at the Royal Institution, April 24, 1866," *Fraser's Magazine* 73 (January–June 1866): 705–16.
8 For a helpful and perceptive introduction to this issue, see Michael R. Emlet, "Prozac and the Promises of God: The Christian Use of Psychoactive Medication," desiringGod (website), August 22, 2019, https://www.desiringgod.org/articles/prozac-and-the-promises-of-god.

a disease has effectively made comfort (complete absence of fear) a health category—or even a moral category. Where discomfort was once considered quite normal (and quite proper for certain situations), it is now deemed an essentially unhealthy thing. It means, for example, that a university student can say, "I am uncomfortable with your views," and consider that a legitimate argument for shutting down further discussion. For it is not acceptable to make someone uncomfortable.

It means that in a culture awash with fear and anxiety, fear is increasingly seen as a *wholly* negative thing in society. And Christians have been swept along in that greater tide of opinion, adopting society's negative assessment of all fear. Small wonder, then, that we shy away from talking about the fear of God, despite its prominence in Scripture and in Christian thought historically. It is completely understandable, but it is tragic: the loss of the fear of God is what ushered in our modern age of anxiety, but the fear of God is the very antidote to our fretfulness.

Speaking a Better Word

In contrast to how things are today, Christians in past generations who embraced the fear of God managed to speak of fear with an enviable combination of tenderness, optimism, and roundedness. An example is John Flavel, one of the last generation of Puritans. In his classic work "A Practical Treatise on Fear," he shows a touching sensitivity to the mental anguish our fears can cause:

> Among all the creatures God hath made (devils only excepted) man is the most apt and able to be his own tormentor; and of all the scourges with which he lasheth and afflicteth both his mind and body, none is found so cruel and intolerable as his own fears.

The worse the times are like to be, the more need the mind hath of succour and encouragement, to confirm and fortify it for hard encounters; but from the worst prospect, fear inflicts the deepest and most dangerous wounds upon the mind of man, cutting the very nerves of its passive fortitude and bearing ability.[9]

Yet rather than being sent by this prospect into a downward spiral of anxiety (like our culture), Flavel is upbeat and helpful. For he has a clear and happy answer. At the root of most of our fears, he argues, is our unbelief:

If men would but dig to the root of their fears, they would certainly find unbelief there, Matth. viii. 26. Why are ye afraid, O ye of little faith! The less faith, still the more fear: Fear is generated by unbelief, and unbelief strengthened by fear; . . . and therefore all the skill in the world can never cure us of the disease of fear, till God first cure us of our unbelief; Christ therefore took the right method to rid his disciples of their fear, by rebuking their unbelief.[10]

Anxiety grows best in the soil of unbelief. It withers in contact with faith. And faith is fertilized by the fear of God, as Flavel demonstrates in the rest of his treatise.

A Rose by Any Other Name Would Smell as Sweet

Flavel saw what we struggle to see today, that not all fear is the same, or bad, or unhealthy, or unpleasant. He argued that we must distinguish between different sorts of fear, between wrong fear and right

---

9 John Flavel, "A Practical Treatise on Fear," in *The Whole Works of John Flavel*, vol. 3 (London: W. Baynes and Son, 1820), 239.

10 Flavel, "A Practical Treatise on Fear," 264.

fear.[11] That is what we will do now as we look at how Scripture details some quite different types of fear—some negative, some positive. For then we can rejoice in the fact that the fear of God commended in Scripture is not to be dismissed for how it sounds like fears that torment us. Then we can appreciate how it is a fear that causes delight to Christ and delight to his people. It is the one positive, wonderful fear that deals with our anxieties.

---

11 Flavel, "A Practical Treatise on Fear," 245.

2

Sinful Fear

WE ALL KNOW FEAR. When you experience fear, your body reacts: you feel the adrenaline release as your heart races, your breathing accelerates, your muscles tense, and your brain goes hyperalert. Sometimes that can be intensely fun: think of the rush of the roller coaster or the big game. Sometimes it can come as a terrifying "amygdala hijack" as panic grips you so utterly, you cannot think but only shake, sweat, and fret.

Underneath those bodily experiences are common thoughts. We fear when we encounter something we cannot control. We fear when we face the prospect of either losing something we love or experiencing something bad. We even fear when we face the prospect of gaining something wonderful, when that thing seems too impossibly wonderful for us. Drilling to the bottom of the matter, the Dutch theologian Wilhelmus à Brakel explained that "fear issues forth from love."[1] That is, we fear *because* we love: we love ourselves and so fear bad things happening to us; we love our families, our friends, our things and so fear losing them.

---

1 Wilhelmus à Brakel, *The Christian's Reasonable Service*, trans. Bartel Elshout, ed. Joel R. Beeke, vol. 3 (Grand Rapids, MI: Reformation Heritage, 1992), 291.

But it is not only that we fear *losing* those things we love; strange to say, we also fear precisely *that which is lovely*. You would expect us to turn away only from ugliness and sights that revolt us. In reality, we also find we must avert our gaze in the face of great beauty, for sheer loveliness can be overwhelming. The bridegroom can dream of staring into his beloved's eyes, and yet find himself at times unable to hold her gaze for love of her beauty. J. R. R. Tolkien once called this "the fear of the beautiful" and explained that it was the very reason he loved the genre of fantasy:

> I desired dragons with a profound desire. Of course, I in my timid body did not wish to have them in the neighbourhood, intruding into my relatively safe world, in which it was, for instance, possible to read stories in peace of mind, free from fear. But the world that contained even the imagination of Fáfnir was richer and more beautiful, at whatever cost of peril.[2]

We don't instinctively recognize that we actually *fear* what is rich and good and beautiful. Yet, as the perilous world of dragons was fearfully attractive to Tolkien, so too can good things be deliciously formidable. That is why the fear of success is often stronger than the fear of failure. Failure and mediocrity can be comfortable and undemanding friends, whereas the prospect of success can be daunting. Our frailty is such that in the face of greatness, vitality, and joy, we can feel it is all too much for us.

Fear also has a tendency to create a groove in our minds: the more we fear something, the more we become engrossed with it and can't let it go. As John Bunyan put it,

2 J. R. R. Tolkien, "On Fairy-Stories," in *Tree and Leaf* (London: George Allen & Unwin, 1964), 40.

All fear, good and bad, hath a natural propenseness in it to incline the heart to contemplate upon the object of fear, and though a man should labour to take off his thoughts from the object of his fear, whether that object was men, hell, devils, &c., yet do what he could the next time his fear had any act in it, it would return again to its object.[3]

Whether we are fascinated or repelled by the object of our fear, there are common traits to all our fears: they arise from what we love, they excite the body, and they can fixate the mind. They have a common DNA.

However, it is equally important to recognize that there are different *sorts* of fear. Confusion on this point is deadly. Take, for example, one Christian reaction to how our culture has cast off the fear of God, and how the church has largely capitulated in removing the fear of God from its vocabulary. Some Christians see the clear lack of reverence and awe of God in our Christian circles and seem to think the answer is to make people *afraid* of God. As if our love for God needs to be tempered by being *afraid* of him.

Scripture speaks quite differently about the fear of God. Take, for example, Exodus 20, where the people of Israel gather at Mount Sinai:

> Now when all the people saw the thunder and the flashes of lightning and the sound of the trumpet and the mountain smoking, the people were afraid and trembled, and they stood far off and said to Moses, "You speak to us, and we will listen; but do not let God speak to us, lest we die." Moses said to the people, "*Do not*

---

3 John Bunyan, "A Treatise on the Fear of God," in *The Works of John Bunyan*, ed. George Offer, 3 vols. (Glasgow: W. G. Blackie & Son, 1854; repr., Edinburgh: Banner of Truth, 1991), 1:463.

fear, for God has come to test you, *that the fear of him may be before you,* that you may not sin." (vv. 18–20)

Moses here sets out a contrast between being *afraid* of God and *fearing* God: those who have the fear of him will not be afraid of him. Yet he uses the same "fear" word root (ירא, *yr'*) for both terms (יָרֵא, *yare' /* יִרְאָה, *yir'ah*). Evidently there are different types of fear. Indeed, there are different types of *fear of God.* There is a fear of God that is good and desirable, and there is a fear of God that is not.

Let's have a look now at the different types of fear we meet in Scripture. That way we can start to clarify our understanding of the very specific fear of God that Scripture commends.

Natural Fear

First, since we live in a fallen world, we live surrounded by danger. The greatest of these dangers is death, "the king of terrors" (Job 18:14). But we also fear accidents, pain, and enemies. For the fall made the world a place full of fear.

That does not mean, though, that our fears of these dangers are themselves sinful. The Gospels tell us how, in the face of his impending death, Jesus was "greatly distressed and troubled" (Mark 14:33)—so greatly, in fact, that in his agony "his sweat became like great drops of blood falling down to the ground" (Luke 22:44).

On top of these natural fears that believers and unbelievers share, Christian theologians have commonly described two other types of fear. More specifically, they have described two different types of *fear of God.* Among the Puritans, for example, John Flavel distinguished between "sinful" and "religious" fear; George Swinnock wrote of "servile" and "filial" fear; William Gurnall, of "slavish" and "holy" fear; and John Bunyan, of "ungodly" and "godly" fear.[4] I will call them "sinful" and "right" fear.

Sinful Fear

The first type of fear of God, "sinful fear," is condemned by Scripture. I have been tempted to call it "wrong fear," but there is a sense in which it is actually quite right for unbelievers to be afraid of God. The holy God *is* terrible to those who are far from him. Instead, I am calling it "sinful fear," since it is a fear of God that flows from sin.

This sinful fear of God is the sort of fear James tells us the demons have when they believe and shudder (James 2:19). It is the fear Moses wanted to remove from the Israelites at Sinai. It is the fear Adam had when he first sinned and hid from God (Gen. 3:10). Adam was the first one to feel this fear, and his reaction in that moment shows us its essential nature: sinful fear drives you *away* from God. This is the fear of the unbeliever who hates God, who remains a rebel at heart, who fears being exposed as a sinner and so runs from God.

This is the fear of God that is at odds with love for God. It is the fear that is, instead, rooted in the very heart of sin. Dreading, opposing, and retreating from God, this fear generates the doubt that rationalizes unbelief. It is the motor for both atheism and idolatry, inspiring people to invent alternative "realities" in place of the living God. Take, for example, the late Christopher Hitchens, one of the "four horsemen" of the early twenty-first-century "New Atheism." Hitchens preferred to describe himself as an "anti-theist" rather than simply an atheist

---

4 John Flavel, "A Practical Treatise on Fear," in *The Whole Works of John Flavel*, vol. 3 (London: W. Baynes and Son, 1820), 245; George Swinnock, *The Works of George Swinnock*, vol. 3 (Edinburgh: James Nichol, 1868; repr., Edinburgh: Banner of Truth, 1992), 295; William Gurnall, *The Christian in Complete Armour*, rev. and abr., 3 vols. (Edinburgh: Banner of Truth, 1986–1989), 1:119, 222, 263, 372, 373; 2:579; Bunyan, "A Treatise on the Fear of God."

because he did not simply deny the existence of God: he was opposed to the very possibility of God's existence. But this anti-theism, he was clear, was motivated by a fear of God. Asked on Fox News what he thought about the possibility of God's existence, he replied:

> I think it would be rather awful if it was true. If there was a permanent, total, round-the-clock divine supervision and invigilation of everything you did, you would never have a waking or sleeping moment when you weren't being watched and controlled and supervised by some celestial entity from the moment of your conception to the moment of your death. . . . It would be like living in North Korea.[5]

Hitchens tragically misunderstood God and so feared God.

The same could be said of the young Martin Luther. Luther once explained how, under the medieval Roman Catholicism he had grown up with,

> Christ was depicted as a grim tyrant, a furious and stern judge who demanded much of us and imposed good works as payment for our sins. . . . This makes us reluctant to go to Him. If my conscience is stricken with fear, I feel sufficiently repelled. . . . My heart and bad conscience quite naturally shun him whom I fear. Fear and terror prod and goad me away from him, so that I do not stay with him.[6]

As a monk Luther found himself utterly terror stricken at the thought of this grim tyrant he thought was in heaven. He was afraid of God,

---

5 Christopher Hitchens, interview on *Hannity & Colmes*, Fox News, May 13, 2007.
6 Martin Luther, *Luther's Works*, vol. 23, *Sermons on the Gospel of St. John: Chapters 6–8*, ed. Jaroslav Jan Pelikan, Hilton C. Oswald, and Helmut T. Lehmann (St. Louis, MO: Concordia, 1999), 57.

filled with a fear that was the very opposite of love. As Luther put it, "I did not love, yes, I hated the righteous God who punishes sinners, and secretly, if not blasphemously, certainly murmuring greatly, I was angry with God."[7] It was only when he felt himself to be born again in the knowledge of Christ as a kind Savior that Luther could say, "He will not be a terror to me, but a comfort."[8]

Misunderstanding God

The experiences of Christopher Hitchens and Martin Luther show that this sinful fear that flees from God arises in good part from a misunderstanding of him. The unfaithful servant in Jesus's parable of the ten minas displays exactly this problem when he unfairly complains to his master, "I was afraid of you, because you are a severe man" (Luke 19:21; see also Matt. 25:24–25). He sees nothing of his master's kindness: in his shortsighted eyes the great man is all parsimonious severity, and therefore the servant is simply afraid. He is just like Adam, who, though once convinced of God's goodness, becomes tempted to think of God as mean-spirited and uncharitably restrictive.

As the Puritan Thomas Manton argued, this is the very myopia Satan loves to inflict on our understanding of God:

Satan laboureth to represent God by halves, only as a consuming fire, as clothed with justice and vengeance. Oh, no! It is true he will not suffer his mercy to be abused by contemptuous sinners; he will not clear the guilty, though he waiteth long on them before he destroyeth them; but the main of his name is "his mercy and

---

7   *Luther's Works*, vol. 34, *Career of the Reformer IV*, 336–37.
8   *Luther's Works*, 23:336.

goodness." Take it as God proclaimeth it, and see if you have any reason to have hard thoughts of God.[9]

Just as it was in the garden, Satan's chief labor is to misrepresent God. He would present him to us as purely negative threat, the embodiment of anti-gospel. For then, when we perceive God as pure threat, we will run from him in fear, wishing that the heavenly ogre did not exist. Stephen Charnock explains:

> When we apprehend a thing hurtful to us, we desire so much evil to it, as may render it incapable of doing us the hurt we fear. As we wish the preservation of what we love or hope for, so we are naturally apt to wish the not being of that whence we fear some hurt or trouble. . . . [The fearful man] wishes God deprived of his being.[10]

Yet while this deception-fueled fear of God drives people away from their Maker, it does not always drive them away from religion. It need not even drive them away from an apparently impressive morality, religious life, and obedience to the law. Having presented God as harsh and dreadful, this fear gives people the mindset of a reluctant slave who obeys his master not out of any love but purely from fear of the whip. Out of slavish fear, people will perform all manner of external duties in order to appease a God they secretly despise. To all the world they can seem devout, exemplary Christians, if rather lacking in joy. So it was with the young Luther, who murmured and raged inwardly while outwardly acting the part of the devoted and obedient monk. These poor slaves can even pontificate on the

---

9   Thomas Manton, *Works of Thomas Manton*, vol. 9 (London: James Nisbet, 1872), 645.
10 Stephen Charnock, *The Works of Stephen Charnock*, 10 vols. (Edinburgh: James Nichol, 1864; repr. Edinburgh: Banner of Truth, 1985), 1:190–91.

forgotten importance of the fear of God—only it is the wrong fear they know. John Colquhoun describes them like this:

> When a man is driven to acts of obedience by the dread of God's wrath revealed in the law and not drawn to them by the belief of His love revealed in the gospel, when he fears God because of His power and justice and not because of His goodness, when he regards God more as an avenging Judge than as a compassionate Friend and Father, and when he contemplates God rather as terrible in majesty than as infinite in grace and mercy, he shows that he is under the dominion or, at least, under the prevalence of a legal spirit.[11]

Colquhoun calls it "a legal spirit"; he could as accurately have said "a sinful fear." Why do people torture themselves with such servile religiosity? John Bunyan answers, "What else is the cause but this ungodly fear?"[12]

When people, through misunderstanding, become simply afraid of God, they will never entrust themselves to him but must turn elsewhere for their security. In fact, it is when people have this confused fear of God that they turn to other gods.

> But every nation still made gods of its own and put them in the shrines of the high places that the Samaritans had made, every nation in the cities in which they lived. The men of Babylon made Succoth-benoth, the men of Cuth made Nergal, the men of Hamath made Ashima, and the Avvites made Nibhaz and Tartak; and the Sepharvites burned their children in the fire to Adrammelech

---

11 John Colquhoun, *Treatise on the Law and Gospel*, ed. D. Kistler (1859; repr., Morgan, PA: Soli Deo Gloria, 1999), 143.

12 Bunyan, "A Treatise on the Fear of God," 448.

and Anammelech, the gods of Sepharvaim. They also feared the LORD and appointed from among themselves all sorts of people as priests of the high places, who sacrificed for them in the shrines of the high places. (2 Kings 17:29–32)

They "feared the LORD"—and served their own gods. Or, it may be that they turn not to other gods but to priests, doctors, or horoscopes. Thus, wrote Calvin,

> When unbelievers transfer the government of the universe from God to the stars, they fancy that their bliss or their misery depends upon the decrees and indications of the stars, not upon God's will; so it comes about that their fear is transferred from him, toward whom alone they ought to direct it, to stars and comets.[13]

Their misguided fear of God thus leads them to a fear of other things, things that cannot liberate or enliven but only enslave and deaden.

Take Stalin's Soviet Union as another example. There, atheistic communism's dread of God did not usher in a humanist idyll as it fled from God and cast off the shackles of Christianity. Without any God-centered rationale for higher beauty and human dignity, a grim dystopia grew in Russia, where life was cheap and boxed in a drab world of grey cement conformity. And another fear was spawned: the terror of the state. It is hard for us today to grasp just how scared out of their wits people were under the constant threat of arbitrary arrest and liquidation or gulag, but we can hear the soundtrack in Dmitri Shostakovich's Tenth Symphony. Creeping, then utterly brutal, it poignantly captures the cold sweaty panic of a purely godless state.

---

13 John Calvin, *Institutes of the Christian Religion*, ed. John T. McNeill, trans. Ford Lewis Battles (Louisville: Westminster John Knox, 2011), 1.16.3.

In other words, this sinful fear of God is a festering sore that spews out an ooze of other toxic fears.

People with this fear of God will not then trust in Christ for their salvation. They will look elsewhere. They will trust the law, their own efforts, or anything or anyone but Christ. Which is why a prophet like Samuel would seek to correct people's *fears*. Take his farewell address to the people of Israel, which is all about the nature of their fear. Samuel had been calling on the people to fear the Lord with a right fear (1 Sam. 12:14). After seeing the Lord's power at work, the people did: they "greatly feared the LORD"(12:18). However, it was the same sort of flinching fear they showed at Sinai. "Pray for your servants to the LORD your God," they asked, "that we may not die" (12:19). Samuel replied:

> *Do not be afraid*; you have done all this evil. Yet do not turn aside from following the LORD, but serve the LORD with all your heart. And do not turn aside after empty things that cannot profit or deliver, for they are empty. For the LORD will not forsake his people, for his great name's sake, because it has pleased the LORD to make you a people for himself. Moreover, as for me, far be it from me that I should sin against the LORD by ceasing to pray for you, and I will instruct you in the good and the right way. *Only fear the Lord* and serve him faithfully with all your heart. (12:20–24)[14]

The Dread of Holiness

Another part of this sinful fear is the fear of letting go of sin, or what we might call the dread of holiness. C. S. Lewis explores this idea in *The*

---

14 Like Moses in Ex. 20, Samuel uses the word root ירא to refer to the Israelites' being afraid in 1 Sam. 12:20 and their having proper fear of the Lord in 1 Sam. 12:24.

Great Divorce, which in many ways is a story about the dread of holiness. Lewis's dream starts in the grey town (hell). While everyone there is afraid of the dark, few dare step aboard the bus to heaven, because they are even more afraid of the light. For, while the darkness is scary in how it shrouds nameless horrors, the light is more so in that it exposes them.

When the bus arrives in the bright beauty of the heavenly meadow, one of the spectral souls from hell screams, "I don't like it! I don't like it. . . . It gives me the pip!"[15] Then the "Solid People"—the residents of heaven—arrive, at which, Lewis writes, "two of the ghosts screamed and ran for the bus."[16] Now in some sense, the solid people and the whole place *mean* to frighten the ghosts, in order to take their minds off themselves. But it is not that the solid people mean any harm. Far from it: they are there only to help. Yet their very splendor is terrifying to the shrunken wraiths from hell.

> "Go away!" squealed the Ghost. "Go away! Can't you see I want to be alone?"
>
> "But you need help," said the Solid One.
>
> "If you have the least trace of decent feeling left," said the Ghost, "you'll keep away. I don't want help. I want to be left alone."[17]

The ghost of the narrator sees another ghost who is "apparently haunted by the terror of discovery. At every whisper of the wind it stopped and cowered: once, at the cry of a bird, it struggled back to its last place of cover."[18] The narrator fears that he simply does not belong in this pure and beautiful place. "Terror whispered, 'This is no place for you.'"[19] The

---

15 C. S. Lewis, *The Great Divorce* (London: Geoffrey Bles, 1946; repr., London: Fount, 1997), 17.

16 Lewis, *The Great Divorce*, 18.

17 Lewis, *The Great Divorce*, 46–47.

18 Lewis, *The Great Divorce*, 37.

19 Lewis, *The Great Divorce*, 46.

fear, for the ghosts, is their realization that to dwell in heaven they must give up their "dignity" or self-dependence, their misery, their anger, their grumbles. They cannot imagine being without the very things that deform them and keep them from happiness, and they shudder at the prospect of liberation and purification. Their sinful fear is a struggle against joy. It is a fear of the light and a refusal to let go of the darkness.

Perhaps the most poignant scene is the one where we see a ghost with a cruel and whispering lizard of lust on his shoulder. An angel offers to kill the lizard and so free the ghost, at which the ghost cries: "Get back! You're burning me. How can I tell you to kill it? You'd kill *me* if you did. . . . Oh, I know. You think I am a coward. But it isn't that. Really it isn't. Let me run back by to-night's bus and get an opinion from my own doctor. I'll come again the first moment I can."[20] When the ghost finally allows the "Burning One" to kill his lust, the lizard is flung down to death on the turf. Then ghost and lizard arise as a complete man and a glorious stallion, silvery white, and the man rides off in glorious freedom and immensity of life. The narrator's teacher (the glorified George MacDonald) concludes that our sinful fears are an erroneous fear of putting sin to death, a fear that fails to understand the glory of the new life to follow in Christ. "Nothing," he says,

> not even the best and noblest, can go on as it now is. Nothing, not even what is lowest and most bestial, will not be raised again if it submits to death. It is sown a natural body, it is raised a spiritual body. Flesh and blood cannot come to the Mountains. Not because they are too rank, but because they are too weak. What is a lizard

20 Lewis, *The Great Divorce*, 83–84.

compared with the stallion? Lust is a poor, weak, whimpering, whispering thing compared with that richness and energy of desire which will arise when lust has been killed.[21]

Yet, as with Tolkein's fantasy world of dragons, it is the very richness and energy of the pure life of heaven that is so overwhelming and fearful to the ghosts. Indeed, they will do almost anything to avoid it. Some of the ghosts even try to terrify heaven by flaunting their own decay and acting as spooky specters. As Tacitus said, "They terrify lest they should fear."[22] Sinners prefer their darkness and their chains to the light and freedom of heaven, and so they dread its holiness. In the words of the real, historical George MacDonald (who was clearly on Lewis's mind as he wrote):

> God must be terrible to those that are far from him; for they fear he will do, yea, he is doing with them what they do not, cannot desire, and can ill endure. Such as many men are, such as all without God would become, they must prefer a devil, because of his supreme selfishness, to a God who will die for his creatures, and insists upon giving himself to them, insists upon their being unselfish and blessed like himself. That which is the power and worth of life they must be, or die; and the vague consciousness of this makes them afraid. They love their poor existence as it is; God loves it as it must be—and they fear him.[23]

Small wonder, then, that our culture is building ever-higher walls to defend itself from the unsettling beauty of God—or even the very

21 Lewis, *The Great Divorce*, 87.
22 Quoted in Lewis, *The Great Divorce*, 63.
23 George MacDonald, *Unspoken Sermons, Second Series* (London: Longmans, Green & Co., 1885), 73–74.

idea of beauty. Traditional conceptions of beauty are being dismissed as discriminatory and nonegalitarian, and all things are declared to be *equally* beautiful. The existence of any absolute beauty is denied as the arts and media simultaneously fear and revel in the perverse, the crooked, and the ugly.

Sinful Fear in Christians

Sadly, Christians are not immune to this sinful fear. Poor teaching, hard times, and Satan's accusations can all cultivate this cringing fear of God in our hearts. What weed killer can we use? Really, the rest of this book is an attempt to hold out the deeper cure. For now, though, here are some golden words of wisdom from John Bunyan. In 1679, the year after he published his *Pilgrim's Progress*, Bunyan produced his remarkable "Treatise on the Fear of God." It is, perhaps, Bunyan's most theologically astute work, and proof that he must have been the most intellectually gifted and pastorally wise tinker the world has ever seen! Seeking to quell any of this ungodly fear that makes people flee from God, Bunyan writes to the reader:

> *Quest.* 1. Do not these fears make thee question whether there was ever a work of grace wrought in thy soul?
> *Answ.* Yes, verily, that they do.

> *Quest.* 2. Do not these fears make thee question whether ever thy first fears were wrought by the Holy Spirit of God?
> *Answ.* Yes, verily, that they do.

> *Quest.* 3. Do not these fears make thee question whether ever thou hast had, indeed, any true comfort from the Word and Spirit of God?
> *Answ.* Yes, verily, that they do.

Quest. 4. Dost thou not find intermixed with these fears plain assertions that thy first comforts were either from thy fancy, or from the devil, and a fruit of his delusions?
Answ. Yes, verily, that I do.

Quest. 5. Do not these fears weaken thy heart in prayer?
Answ. Yes, that they do.

Quest. 6. Do not these fears keep thee back from laying hold of the promise of salvation by Jesus Christ?
Answ. Yes; for I think if I were deceived before, if I were comforted by a spirit of delusion before, why may it not be so again? so I am afraid to take hold of the promise.

Quest. 7. Do not these fears tend to the hardening of thy heart, and to the making of thee desperate?
Answ. Yes, verily, that they do.

Quest. 8. Do not these fears hinder thee from profiting in hearing or reading of the Word?
Answ. Yes, verily, for still whatever I hear or read, I think nothing that is good belongs to me.

Quest. 9. Do not these fears tend to the stirring up of blasphemies in thy heart against God?
Answ. Yes, to the almost distracting of me.

Quest. 10. Do not these fears make thee sometimes think, that it is in vain for thee to wait upon the Lord any longer?
Answ. Yes, verily; and I have many times almost come to this conclusion, that I will read, pray, hear, company with God's people, or the like, no longer.

Well, poor Christian, I am glad that thou hast so plainly answered me; but, prithee [i.e., please], look back upon thy answer. How much of God dost thou think is in these things? how much of his Spirit, and the grace of his Word? Just none at all; for it cannot be that these things can be the true and natural effects of the workings of the Spirit of God: no, not as a spirit of bondage. These are not his doings. Dost thou not see the very paw of the devil in them?[24]

It is, Bunyan says, the devil's work to promote a fear of God that makes people afraid of God such that they want to flee from God. The Spirit's work is the exact opposite: to produce in us a wonderful fear that wins and draws us *to* God. It is to this happy, Scripture-commended, Spirit-breathed fear that we turn now.

---

24 Bunyan, "A Treatise on the Fear of God," 452.

3

Right Fear

C. I. SCOFIELD ONCE CALLED *the fear of God* "a phrase of Old Testament piety."[1] And so indeed it was. However, *the fear of God* is not a phrase of Old Testament piety *only*, for the right fear of God is, quite explicitly, a blessing of the new covenant. Speaking of the new covenant, the Lord promised through Jeremiah:

> And they shall be my people, and I will be their God. I will give them one heart and one way, that they may fear me forever, for their own good and the good of their children after them. I will make with them an everlasting covenant, that I will not turn away from doing good to them. *And I will put the fear of me in their hearts, that they may not turn from me.* (Jer. 32:38–40)

What is this fear that the Lord will put in the hearts of his people in the new covenant? Unlike that devilish fear we have seen that would drive us away from God, this is a fear that keeps us from drawing back or turning away from him. Is it, then, the sort of "spirit of slavery" (Rom. 8:15) that John Newton wrote of in his hymn "Amazing Grace"?

---

1   *Scofield Reference Bible*, 1909 ed., 607n1.

'Twas grace that taught my heart to fear,
And grace my fears relieved.

Well, certainly, the Spirit can cause a fear in those he is convicting of sin, a fear that drives them to Christ for refuge. But, as Newton said, that fear is then *relieved* by grace: it is no longer appropriate for a believer once he or she has trusted in Christ. It is a Spirit-worked fear that serves a good purpose in driving sinners to Christ; it is not, however, that fear which is "the soul of godliness"[2] or "the beginning of wisdom" (Prov. 9:10).

An Unexpected Fear

In Jeremiah 33, the Lord goes on to explain the nature of this new covenant fear in words so striking they overturn all our expectations. He promises:

> I will cleanse them from all the guilt of their sin against me, and I will forgive all the guilt of their sin and rebellion against me. And this city shall be to me a name of joy, a praise and a glory before all the nations of the earth who shall hear of all the good that I do for them. They shall fear and tremble *because of all the good and all the prosperity I provide for it.* (vv. 8–9)

This is not a fear of punishment—of what God might do if his people turn away from him. Quite the opposite: in Jeremiah 33, the Lord reels off a catalog of pure blessing.[3] He will cleanse them, forgive them, and do great good for them. And they fear and tremble precisely *because of* all the good he does for them.

---

2 John Murray, *Principles of Conduct: Aspects of Biblical Ethics* (London: Tyndale, 1957), 229.
3 See also Ps. 67:7 as the climax of the chiastic Ps. 67.

Here is not a fear that stands on the flip side of the grace and goodness of God. It is the sort of fear Hosea describes when he prophesies how "the children of Israel shall return and seek the LORD their God, and David their king, *and they shall come in fear to the* LORD *and to his goodness in the latter days*" (Hos. 3:5). It is a fear "*to* the LORD and *to* his goodness." It is a fear that, as Charles Spurgeon put it, "leans toward the Lord" *because of* his very goodness.[4] It is the sort of marveling fear we come across in the face of Jesus's giving of life. When Jesus raised the widow of Nain's son, we read,

Then he came up and touched the bier, and the bearers stood still. And he said, "Young man, I say to you, arise." And the dead man sat up and began to speak, and Jesus gave him to his mother. Fear seized them all, and they glorified God, saying, "A great prophet has arisen among us!" and "God has visited his people!" (Luke 7:14–16)

Take another surprising example of this fear, from when the Lord appears to Jacob at Bethel. As in Jeremiah 33, the Lord utters not one word of threat but only promise after promise of pure grace:

Jacob left Beersheba and went toward Haran. And he came to a certain place and stayed there that night, because the sun had set. Taking one of the stones of the place, he put it under his head and lay down in that place to sleep. And he dreamed, and behold, there was a ladder set up on the earth, and the top of it reached to heaven. And behold, the angels of God were ascending and descending on it! And behold, the LORD stood above it and said, "I am the LORD, the God of Abraham your father and the God

---

4 C. H. Spurgeon, "A Fear to Be Desired," in *The Metropolitan Tabernacle Pulpit Sermons*, 63 vols. (London: Passmore & Alabaster, 1855–1917), 48:495.

of Isaac. The land on which you lie I will give to you and to your offspring. Your offspring shall be like the dust of the earth, and you shall spread abroad to the west and to the east and to the north and to the south, and in you and your offspring shall all the families of the earth be blessed. Behold, I am with you and will keep you wherever you go, and will bring you back to this land. For I will not leave you until I have done what I have promised you." Then Jacob awoke from his sleep and said, "Surely the LORD is in this place, and I did not know it." And he was afraid and said, "How awesome [fearful] is this place! This is none other than the house of God, and this is the gate of heaven." (Gen. 28:10–17)

The Lord promises to bless and increase Jacob, to be with him and to keep him, never to leave him, and to fulfill all his good purposes for him. And in the face of pure goodness and absolute grace, Jacob *fears*. As the Puritan William Gouge explains, true godly fear actually "arises from faith in the mercy and goodness of God: for when the heart of man hath once felt a sweet taste of God's goodness, and found that in his favour only all happiness consisteth, it is stricken with such an inward awe and reverence."[5]

Here I need to add a caveat: Gouge describes the fear of God here as "an inward awe and reverence," and it is common for Christians to use "awe," "respect," and "reverence" as *synonyms* for the fear of God. Certainly that is a *part* of the Christian's right fear of God, and fits to some extent with the fact that in Scripture people fall on their faces as though dead before God. However, I hope we will come to see that those words actually fall quite short of capturing the intense and happy fullness of what Scripture means when it speaks of the fear of God.

5   William Gouge, *Domesticall Duties* (London: John Beale, 1626), 5.

What we can already say, though, is that the fear of God commended in Scripture "does not arise from a perception of God as hazardous, but glorious. In other words, it flows from an appreciation of God."[6] It can come as quite a shock to see the God who is love described as "the Fear." But in Genesis, when briefly listing some divine titles, Jacob speaks to Laban of "the God of my Father, the God of Abraham and *the Fear of Isaac*" (Gen. 31:42; see also v. 53). This startling title speaks of the profound impression left upon Jacob by his father's faith. Evidently, Jacob had been taught that the Lord God is so intrinsically "fearful" by nature and identity that he can be known simply as "the Fear." (And in Ps. 19, among the various descriptions of the word of God—the "law of the LORD," "the testimony of the LORD," "the precepts of the LORD," "the commandment of the LORD," and "the rules of the LORD"—we see Scripture described as "the fear of the LORD" [vv. 7–9]. The word of God so perfectly manifests the glory of "the Fear" that it is itself fearful.)

But what could Isaac have meant by describing his God as "the Fear"? What do we know of his experience of God that could help us understand this extraordinary title? As it turns out, the overwhelming impression left by his story in Genesis is that Isaac was repeatedly the recipient of undeserved grace. Even before his birth, Isaac was the child of promise, the fruit of grace. He was the son who would inherit (Gen. 21). He was rescued by the angel of the Lord and atoned for (Gen. 22). For him, the Lord provided a wonderful wife in an extraordinary way (Gen. 24). Then, after the death of Abraham, we read, "God blessed Isaac his son" (Gen. 25:11). Later in that same chapter: "Isaac prayed to the LORD for his wife, because she was barren. And

---

6 J. Stephen Yuille, *Looking unto Jesus: The Christ-Centered Piety of Seventeenth-Century Baptists* (Cambridge: Lutterworth, 2014), xviii.

the LORD granted his prayer, and Rebekah his wife conceived" (Gen. 25:21). "And Isaac sowed in that land and reaped in the same year a hundredfold. The LORD blessed him" (Gen. 26:12). What else can we conclude but that Isaac, like Jacob, knew a God who was fearfully gracious? All the evidence suggests that he feared and trembled *because of* all the good the Lord provided for him (just as we find in Jer. 33:8–9).

Looking at the biblical evidence, John Bunyan concluded that those who have no faith will have no true fear of God, those who have a devil's faith will have a devil's fear, and those who have a saint's faith will have a saint's fear. And this godly fear, he explained, flows primarily

> from a sense of the love and kindness of God to the soul . . . from some sense or hope of mercy from God by Jesus Christ. . . . Indeed nothing can lay a stronger obligation upon the heart to fear God, than sense of, or hope in mercy (Jer 33:8, 9). This begetteth true tenderness of heart, true godly softness of spirit; this truly endeareth the affections to God; and in this true tenderness, softness, and endearedness of affection to God, lieth the very essence of this fear of the Lord.[7]

Fear and Love

Clearly, the fear of God is not at all what we, with our culture's allergic reaction to the very concept of fear, might expect. Instead, we can say with Spurgeon that this is the "sort of fear which has in it the very essence of love, and without which there would be no joy even in the presence of God."[8] In fact, the closer we look, the closer fear of God and love of God appear. Sometimes fear of God and love of God are put in parallel, as in Psalm 145:

---

7 John Bunyan, "A Treatise on the Fear of God," in *The Works of John Bunyan*, ed. George Offer, 3 vols. (Glasgow: W. G. Blackie & Son, 1854; repr., Edinburgh: Banner of Truth, 1991), 1:460–61.

8 Spurgeon, "A Fear to Be Desired," 494.

He fulfills the desire of *those who fear him*;
    he also hears their cry and saves them.
The Lord preserves *all who love him*,
    but all the wicked he will destroy. (vv. 19–20)

Similarly, think of how Moses equates fear and love in his summary of the law.

> Now this is the commandment—the statutes and the rules—that the Lord your God commanded me to teach you, that you may do them in the land to which you are going over, to possess it, *that you may fear the Lord your God*. . . .
>
> Hear, O Israel: The Lord our God, the Lord is one. *You shall love the Lord your God* with all your heart and with all your soul and with all your might. (Deut. 6:1–5)

The reason it is not immediately obvious to us that fear and love are so comparable is that we easily misunderstand love. *Love* is a word bandied around in our lives. I "love" sitting in a cozy armchair reading a good book; I "love" my family; I "love" a good laugh with my friends. And so I can blithely assume that "love" for God is just more of the same, meaning nothing more than a (perhaps vague) predilection or preference. Where some enjoy pudding, I enjoy God.

However, my love for one thing differs from my love for another because love changes according to its object. Indeed, the nature of a love is defined by its object. Let me illustrate with three true statements:

1. I love and have real affection for my dog.
2. I love and have real affection for my wife.
3. I love and have real affection for my God.

Each is true, but reading them together like that should make you wince. You know there must be something terribly wrong if I mean exactly the same thing in each. You sincerely hope there is a difference. And there is: the three *loves* differ because the *objects* of the loves differ.

The living God is infinitely perfect and quintessentially, overwhelmingly beautiful in every way: his righteousness, his graciousness, his majesty, his mercy, his all. And so we do not love him aright if our love is not a trembling, overwhelmed, and fearful love. In a sense, then, the trembling "fear of God" is a way of speaking about the intensity of the saints' love for and enjoyment of all that God is. The Puritan William Bates expressed it like this: "There is nothing more fearful than an ingenuous love, and nothing more loving than a filial fear."[9] Similarly, Spurgeon could say:

> It is not because we are afraid of him, but because we delight in him, that we fear before him. . . . "Thine heart shall fear, and be enlarged," says the prophet Isaiah [Isa. 60:5], and so it comes to pass with us. The more we fear the Lord, the more we love him, until this becomes to us the true fear of God, to love him with all our heart, and mind, and soul, and strength.[10]

The right fear of God, then, is not the flip side to our love for God. That kind of thinking was articulated by the Roman Catholic theologian Hans Urs von Balthasar when he argued that "the gospel of grace appear[s] not only as *love* (which is what it is in God) but also as law and command, as reverence, *religio*, distance and fear of the Lord."[11] But

9 William Bates, "On the Fear of God," in *The Whole Works of the Rev. W. Bates*, vol. 3 (London: James Black, 1815), 187.

10 Spurgeon, "A Fear to Be Desired," 498.

11 Hans Urs von Balthasar, *The Theology of Karl Barth*, trans. Edward Oakes (San Francisco: Ignatius, 1992), 287.

Moses's command to Israel in summarizing the law was precisely that God's people should *fear and love* the Lord their God. Right fear does not stand in tension with love for God. Right fear falls on its face before the Lord, but falls leaning "*toward the Lord.*"[12] It is not as if love draws near and fear distances. Nor is this fear of God one side of our reaction to God. It is not simply that we love God for his graciousness and fear him for his majesty. That would be a lopsided fear of God. We also love him in his holiness and tremble at the marvelousness of his mercy. True fear of God is true love for God defined: it is the right response to God's full-orbed revelation of himself in all his grace and glory.

Evidently, the fear that Christ himself has (Isa. 11:1–3), and shares with us, is the opposite of being afraid of God. Godly fear casts out being afraid. But neither is it a cool, passionless regard of God. Time and again we have seen in Scripture that believers who have a godly fear tremble before God. Overwhelmed by his goodness and majesty and holiness and grace and righteousness—by all that God is—the faithful tremble. The biblical theme of the fear of God helps us to see the *sort* of love toward God that is fitting. It shows us that God does not want passionless performance or a vague preference for him. To encounter the living, holy, and all-gracious God truly means that we cannot contain ourselves. He is not a truth to be known unaffectedly, or a good to be received listlessly. Seen clearly, the dazzling beauty and splendor of God must cause our hearts to quake.

To appreciate something of this, take a moment to enjoy the following poem by the hymnwriter F. W. Faber (1814–1863). Entitled "The Fear of God," it is a paean to fear as the intense ecstasy of love:

---

12 Spurgeon, "A Fear to Be Desired," 495, my emphasis.

My fear of Thee, O Lord! exults
Like life within my veins,—
A fear which rightly claims to be
One of love's sacred pains.

Thy goodness to Thy saints of old
An awful thing appeared;
For were Thy majesty less good
Much less would it be feared.

There is no joy the soul can meet
Upon life's various road
Like the sweet fear that sits and shrinks
Under the eye of God.

A special joy is in all love
For objects we revere;
Thus joy in God will always be
Proportioned to our fear.

Oh Thou art greatly to be feared,
Thou art so prompt to bless!
The dread to miss such love as Thine
Makes fear but love's excess.

The fulness of Thy mercy seems
To fill both land and sea
If we can break through bounds so vast,
How exiled shall we be!

For grace is fearful, which each hour
Our path in life has crossed;
If it were rarer, it might be
Less easy to be lost.

But fear is love, and love is fear,
And in and out they move;
But fear is an intenser joy
Than mere unfrightened love.

When most I fear Thee, Lord! then most
Familiar I appear;
And I am in my soul most free,
When I am most in fear.

I should not love Thee as I do,
If love might make more free;
Its very sweetness would be lost
In greater liberty.

I feel Thee most a Father when
I fancy Thee most near;
And Thou comest not so nigh in love
As Thou comest, Lord! in fear.

They love Thee little, if at all,
Who do not fear Thee much;
If love is Thine attraction, Lord!
Fear is Thy very touch.

Love could not love Thee half so much
If it found Thee not so near;
It is thy nearness, which makes love
The perfectness of fear.

We fear because Thou art so good,
And because we can sin;
And when we make most show of love,
We are trembling most within.

And Father! when to us in heaven
Thou shalt Thy Face unveil,
Then more than ever will our souls
Before Thy goodness quail.

Our blessedness will be to bear
The sight of Thee so near,
And thus eternal love will be
But the ecstasy of fear.[13]

Is *Fear* the Best Word?

In all this, a rather important question has begun to rear its head: Is *fear* the most helpful word for this right response to God? This right fear of God is a most positive thing, but it is hard for us to see that, given how wholly negative the word *fear* seems. No wonder Christians—as we noted before—have come to prefer substituting words like *awe*, *respect*, and *reverence* in place of *fear*. So, would another word capture this experience better?

Let's start with the words used in Scripture for fear of God. In Old Testament Hebrew, two word roots are used to describe the *right* fear of God. These both present the Old Testament view of fear and serve as the template for New Testament usage, which translates them with φόβος/φοβέω (*phobos/phobeō*; see, for example, Paul's use of Ps. 36:1 in Rom. 3:18).

The first and most common word root used is ירא (*yr'*). And perhaps what is most striking is how it is used for *both* right *and* sinful fears. We have seen an example of this in Exodus, when "Moses said

---

13 F. W. Faber, "The Fear of God," in *Faber's Hymns* (New York: Thomas Y. Crowell & Co., 1894), 101.

to the people, '*Do not fear*, for God has come to test you, *that the fear of him may be before you*, that you may not sin'" (Ex. 20:18–20). It is used to describe being afraid, as when Adam tells the Lord God, "I heard the sound of you in the garden, and *I was afraid*, because I was naked, and I hid myself" (Gen. 3:10). But it is also used positively to describe the blessed and awesome graciousness of God:

> *Awesome* is God from his sanctuary;
>> the God of Israel—he is the one who gives power and
>> strength to his people.
> Blessed be God! (Ps. 68:35)

The fact that the same word root can be used both positively and negatively is telling and suggests a commonality between these otherwise very different fears. The other word root helps us understand what that common feature is—and it is most revealing.

This second word root is פחד (*phd*), and like ירא (*yr'*) it is used for both right and sinful fears: anything from bone-melting dread to ecstatic jubilation. It is used negatively:

> The sinners in Zion are *afraid*;
>> trembling has seized the godless. (Isa. 33:14)

And it is used positively: "This city shall be to me a name of joy, a praise and a glory before all the nations of the earth who shall hear of all the good that I do for them. *They shall fear* and tremble because of all the good and all the prosperity I provide for it" (Jer. 33:9). So, what is the common feature that enables the same word to be used for such diametrically opposed experiences? As both those verses help us see, פחד (*phd*) suggests a physical experience: of being overwhelmed, of weak-kneed trembling, of being staggeringly discomposed. Now, I can tremble in quite different ways. I can shake in terror, as a soldier might under heavy fire. But I can also quake in overwhelmed adoration, as when the bridegroom first sees his bride. For another example of פחד (*phd*) involving such happy trembling, see Isaiah 60:5:

> Then you shall see and be radiant;
>> your heart shall *thrill* [פחד (*phd*)] and exult,
> because the abundance of the sea shall be turned to you,
>> the wealth of the nations shall come to you.

What both ירא (*yr'*) and פחד (*phd*) show is that, if we are to be faithful to Scripture's presentation of the fear of God, we should ideally use words that encompass that spectrum of positive and negative experience. What פחד in particular helps us see is the common feature of those fears: trembling. It shows us that the fear of God is no mild-mannered, reserved, or limp thing. It is a startlingly physical, overpowering reaction. And so, *respect* and *reverence* are simply too weak and grey to stand in as synonyms for the fear of God. *Awe* seems a much better fit, though even it doesn't quite capture the physical intensity, the happy thrill, or the exquisite delight that leans toward, instead of away from, the Lord. In fact, these other words can be actively misleading, making us think of this right fear as a response to only certain qualities of God and not others. For example, if we simply use the word *awe*, we will tend to think of fear as a response to only God's transcendence and power, not his graciousness. Or take the word *respect*: it is a strange term for a response to God's love—and so it is an unbalanced substitute for the word *fear*. Similarly, *reverence* can sound too stiff and unresponsive. Not that these are wrong words—it is simply that they are not perfect synonyms for the fear of God.

Perhaps, then, as we seek to speak of the fear of God, it is best to recognize the shortcomings of all words in isolation. The word *fear* has its own baggage to be sure, but it is well established, and no one word can adequately and completely replace it. If people are to appreciate how the fear of God is distinct from all other fears, synonyms alone will not do: it must be unfolded and taught.

Fear and Joy

Speaking of the happy thrill and exquisite delight of this fear is surprising language. Yet Scripture is clear that just as the fear of God defines true love for God, so it defines true joy in God. In the same way that Christ's delight is in the fear of the Lord, so the fear of the Lord is a *pleasure* to believers, for it is about enjoying his fearfully lovely glory.

The living God is not moderately happy but fearfully happy, and when we have this fear, we enter into the joy of our Master. "Blessed" or "happy"—like God—"is the one who fears the LORD always" (Prov. 28:14; see also Isa. 66:5). Thus Nehemiah prays, "O Lord, let your ear be attentive to the prayer of your servant, and to the prayer of your servants who *delight to fear your name*" (Neh. 1:11). Those who "serve the LORD with fear" will "rejoice with trembling" (Ps. 2:11), just as the two women, having heard of the resurrection of Jesus, departed from the tomb "with fear and great joy" (Matt. 28:8). For those who see the glory of the Lord revealed—especially in his mighty acts of salvation—see that he is "awesome" or "fearful" in his glory (Ex. 15:11). That is why Isaiah 60:5 uses פחד (*phd*) ("Then you shall see and be radiant; / your heart shall *thrill* and exult") to describe a joyful emotion where the heart throbs with pleasure. Believers, said Charles Spurgeon, adore and worship the living God "with a joyful, tender fear, which both lays us low, and lifts us very high, for never do we seem to be nearer to heaven's golden throne than when our spirit gives itself up to worship him whom it does not see, but in whose realized presence it trembles with sacred delight."[14]

---

14 Spurgeon, "A Fear to Be Desired," 496.

Because this fear finds a heartfelt delight in God himself, it begins to find a genuine pleasure in walking in his ways. The "man who fears the LORD" will be the very one "who greatly delights in his commandments" (Ps. 112:1). And at the same time, God finds a delight in those who have this trembling, exquisite pleasure in him.

> His delight is not in the strength of the horse,
>> nor his pleasure in the legs of a man,
> but the LORD takes pleasure in those who fear him,
>> in those who hope in his steadfast love. (Ps. 147:10–11)

Puritan preachers were quite often drawn to clarify the nature of this fear of God, and in good part because of how their people were prone to see fear as the opposite of enjoyment. William Ames, for example, distinguished between sinful fear and commendable fear. Sinful fear, he explained, is that "fear which scares men away from God, or which drives them to fly away from him. The fear of them also which are only afraid of Gods anger." In contrast, the fear that Scripture commends is that where "the principal cause of our fear is not any evil which we are in danger of, but *the excellent perfection of God*."[15] For this, as the Puritans saw, is how the Scriptures speak. In Jeremiah 2 the Lord describes himself as the spring of living waters, lamenting that

> my people have committed two evils:
> they have forsaken me,
>> the fountain of living waters,
> and hewed out cisterns for themselves,
>> broken cisterns that can hold no water. (v. 13)

---

15 William Ames, "Conscience with the Power and Cases Thereof," in *The Workes of the Reverend and Faithfull Minister of Christ William Ames* (London: John Rothwell, 1643), 51, my emphasis. In this quotation I have silently updated the spelling.

But what does it mean to forsake the fountain of living waters? The Lord goes on to explain:

> Know and see that it is evil and bitter
>> for you to forsake the LORD your God;
>> *the fear of me is not in you,*
>>>> declares the Lord GOD of hosts. (v. 19)

To fear the Lord is to enjoy him and drink of his sweet water. That is the ultimate sense in which the Lord "is to be feared above all gods" (Ps. 96:4).

This right fear of God, then, is not the minor-key, gloomy flip side to proper joy in God. There is no tension between this fear and joy. Rather, this trembling "fear of God" is a way of speaking about the sheer intensity of the saints' happiness in God. In other words, the biblical theme of the fear of God helps us to see the *sort* of joy that is most fitting for believers. Our desire for God and delight in him are not intended to be lukewarm. As our love for God is a trembling and wonder-filled love, so our joy in God is, *at its purest*, a trembling and wonder-filled—yes, fearful—joy. For the object of our joy is so overwhelmingly and fearfully wonderful. We are made to rejoice and tremble before God, to love and enjoy him with an intensity that is fitting for him. And what more befits his infinite magnificence than an enjoyment of him that is more than our frail selves can bear, which overwhelms us and causes us to tremble? Normally our joy in God is cold and tarnished, but as we work out our salvation "with fear and trembling" (Phil. 2:12), we become ever more fearfully happy, like our God.

This extraordinary pairing of joy with fear can be seen well when two wise and famous statements are put together. One speaks of "the whole duty of man," the other of "man's chief end," but both are about the same thing: the purpose for which we were made. The first statement is from the book of Ecclesiastes where the Preacher concludes his argument: "The end of the matter; all has been heard. Fear God and keep his commandments, for this is the whole duty of man" (Eccles. 12:13). The second statement is the first answer from the Westminster Shorter Catechism, which tells us, "Man's chief end is to glorify God, and to enjoy him forever." Should we fear God and keep his commandments or glorify God and enjoy him forever? There is no contradiction, for they are describing the same truth. Those who fear God glorify him, as they sing the song of the victorious in Revelation 15:4:

> Who will not fear, O Lord,
>   and glorify your name?

Not only that: when the Preacher calls us to fear God, he is calling us precisely to the exquisite and glorifying enjoyment of God that Westminster calls the chief end of man.

William Bates picked up on this when he set out to examine "the consistency that is between the fear of God, and faith, love, hope and joy."[16] Each, he explained, is an aspect of the one work of grace in the soul, and therefore fear cannot be contrary to joy. Far from it, Bates went on, for the soul will "most kindly rejoice in God, when it is filled with an awful admiration of his goodness; for this fear doth not contract the heart as grief doth, but enlargeth the heart in God's praises."[17]

The point is not that God's goodness alone overwhelms us in our enjoyment of him. Believers will rejoice and tremble at *all* God is. Sometimes in Scripture it is the goodness of God that draws out the

16 Bates, "On the Fear of God," 183.
17 Bates, "On the Fear of God," 188.

fear-filled worship of God's people: "Only fear the LORD and serve him faithfully with all your heart. For consider what great things he has done for you" (1 Sam. 12:24). At other times, though, it is the wisdom of God that has the same effect:

> Who would not fear you, O King of the nations?
>> For this is your due;
> for among all the wise ones of the nations
>> and in all their kingdoms
>> there is none like you. (Jer. 10:7)

Sometimes it is the holiness of God:

> Who will not fear, O Lord,
>> and glorify your name?
> For you alone are holy. (Rev. 15:4)

Sometimes it is his greatness:

> And now, Israel, what does the LORD your God require of you, but to fear the LORD your God, to walk in all his ways, to love him, to serve the LORD your God with all your heart and with all your soul. . . . For the LORD your God is God of gods and Lord of lords, the great, the mighty, and the awesome God, who is not partial and takes no bribe. (Deut. 10:12, 17)

And at other times his forgiveness is what causes us to tremble:

> But with you there is forgiveness,
>> that you may be feared. (Ps. 130:4)

In each case, believers are *enjoying* these beautiful perfections of God. It is not that some of his attributes cause us to love and enjoy him, while others cause us to flinch. As Stephen Charnock explains:

Nothing of God looks terrible in Christ to a believer. The sun is risen, shadows are vanished, God walks upon the battlements of love, justice hath left its sting in a Saviour's side, the law is disarmed, weapons out of his hand, his bosom open, his bowels yearn, his heart pants, sweetness and love is in all his carriage. And this is life eternal, to know God believingly in the glories of his mercy and justice in Jesus Christ.[18]

This indeed is why we search the Scriptures, that we may know God better in all his ways and all his perfections—and might rejoice in him so intensely that we tremble.

> My son, if you receive my words
>   and treasure up my commandments with you,
> making your ear attentive to wisdom
>   and inclining your heart to understanding;
> yes, if you call out for insight
>   and raise your voice for understanding,
> if you seek it like silver
>   and search for it as for hidden treasures,
> then you will understand the fear of the LORD
>   and find the knowledge of God. (Prov. 2:1–5)

The Essence of the New Heart

If fear really is so basic to the life of the believer, we might wonder why it is not listed among the fruit of the Spirit. That fruit, writes Paul to the Galatians, is "love, joy, peace, patience, kindness, goodness, faithfulness, gentleness, self-control" (5:22–23). Love and joy

---

18 Stephen Charnock, *The Complete Works of Stephen Charnock*, 10 vols. (Edinburgh: James Nichol, 1865), 4:163.

he mentions, but not fear. John Bunyan, calling fear the Christian's "highest duty," explains: "It is, as I may call it, not only a duty in itself, but, as it were, the salt that seasoneth every duty. For there is no duty performed by us that can by any means be accepted of God, if it be not seasoned with godly fear."[19] That is, this right fear of God is part of the underlying grain of the new heart. The fruit of the Spirit is precisely that character which grows out of a God-fearing heart. Love, joy, peace, patience, kindness, goodness, faithfulness, gentleness, and self-control are the beautiful, lived embodiment of the fear of God.

That is why fear is not listed there by Paul. One could as well ask why he does not mention faith. For, like fear, faith is part of the new heart's very constitution. The Lord promised through Jeremiah concerning the new covenant, "I will put the fear of me in their hearts, that they may not turn from me" (Jer. 32:40). The new heart that the Spirit gives in regenerating believers is a heart that rejoices with trembling before God, and so a heart that trusts him and does not turn from him.

Right fear is at the heart of holiness, making the difference between hypocritical performance and genuine knowledge of God. It is part of the makeup of the heart that trusts God, which is why we read in Scripture of this fear moving or giving birth to faith. The Israelites, for example, "saw the great power that the LORD used against the Egyptians, so the people feared the LORD, and they believed in the LORD and in his servant Moses" (Ex. 14:31). Those who fear the word of the Lord listen to the word of the Lord (Ex. 9:20–25; Heb. 11:7). In fact, saving faith cannot be separated from the right fear of God, for we will trust in God only to the extent that we have this fear that

19 Bunyan, "A Treatise on the Fear of God," 438.

leans toward him. Fear not only defines our love for God and our joy in God. It also prompts us to trust in God. Thus, John Calvin could write, "The knowledge of God set forth for us in Scripture . . . invites us first to fear God, then to trust in him."[20] The order is inescapable, for only a God-fearing heart will ever be a God-trusting heart.

And therein lies great encouragement. It is second nature to us to build our self-worth upon our performance. Thus a deep despondency can grip the Christian who feels unable to be useful, who is aging in a nursing home or trapped in an apparently mundane job. But "the LORD takes pleasure in those who fear him" (Ps. 147:11). Always. Blessed, therefore, are those who fear God. For, as Bunyan put it:

> God hath not laid the comfort of his people in the doing of external duties, nor the salvation of their souls, but in believing, loving, and fearing God. Neither hath he laid these things in actions done in their health nor in the due management of their most excellent parts, but in the receiving of Christ, and fear of God. The which, good Christian, thou mayest do, and do acceptably, even though thou shouldest lie bed-rid all thy days; thou mayest also be sick and believe; be sick and love, be sick and fear God, and so be a blessed man. And here the poor Christian hath something to answer them that reproach him for his ignoble pedigree, and shortness of the glory of the wisdom of the world. True, may that man say, I was taken out of the dunghill, I was born in a base and low estate, but I fear God. I have no worldly greatness, nor excellency of natural parts, but I fear God.[21]

---

20 John Calvin, *Institutes of the Christian Religion*, ed. John T. McNeill, trans. Ford Lewis Battles (Louisville: Westminster John Knox, 2011), 1.10.2.
21 Bunyan, "A Treatise on the Fear of God," 490.

The flip side to this, of course, is a great challenge. The Lord looks on the heart and is pleased when he finds it quaking in wonder, love, and praise. But that should concern all who place their stock in their outward usefulness rather than the inner state of their hearts.

Yet all should be encouraged. For the nature of the living God means that the fear which pleases him is not a groveling, shrinking fear. He is no tyrant. It is an ecstasy of love and joy that senses how overwhelmingly kind and magnificent, good and true God is, and that therefore leans on him in staggered praise and faith.

4

Overwhelmed by the Creator

THERE ARE DIFFERENT SORTS of fear, then: some good and enjoyable, some bad and terrifying; there is a right fear of God, and there is a sinful fear of God. But if you start to press in, it starts to become clear that there are even more sorts of fear: different *sorts* of *right* fear of God. Forgive me if it sounds like we're about to leave the fairway and head off into the long grass to fuss over little distinctions. Far from it: we're about to go further up and further in.

John Calvin can help set the stage here. In 1559, Calvin produced his final, definitive edition of his masterwork, the *Institutes of the Christian Religion*. People sometime think of Calvin's *Institutes* as an encyclopedia of the faith, and you *can* use it like that, as a dive-in reference book. Calvin, however, wrote it as a flowing argument showing the proper development of a true knowledge of God. He made this argument in four steps:

- Book 1: The Knowledge of God the Creator
- Book 2: The Knowledge of God the Redeemer in Christ
- Book 3: The Way in Which We Receive the Grace of Christ
- Book 4: The External Means or Aids by Which God Invites Us into the Society of Christ and Holds Us Therein

Only the first two steps of his argument are really relevant here, but they are wonderfully clarifying. There are, says Calvin, two steps or levels to our knowledge of God: the knowledge of God the Creator and the knowledge of God the Redeemer in Christ. With this, Calvin has given us a useful template. Just as there are two levels of knowledge of God, so there are two corresponding right fear responses to God: fear of God the Creator and fear of God the Redeemer in Christ.

"O Lord, How Majestic Is Your Name in All the Earth!"

The first sort of right fear is the weak-kneed and trembling response to the fact that God is the Creator. It appreciates—indeed, it enjoys—that God is splendid in his transcendence, above and beyond creation. God is holy, majestic, perfect, all-powerful, and dazzling in all his perfections. This fear considers the Creator and is left staggered, like David, asking, "What is man that you are mindful of him?" (Ps. 8:4). In the light of God's eternal magnificence, self-existence, and unswerving constancy, this fear feels what fleeting and fickle little things we humans are. Calvin wrote:

> Hence that dread and wonder with which Scripture commonly represents the saints as stricken and overcome whenever they felt the presence of God. Thus it comes about that we see men who in his absence normally remained firm and constant, but who, when he manifests his glory, are so shaken and struck dumb as to be laid low by the dread of death—are in fact overwhelmed by it and almost annihilated. As a consequence, we must infer that man is never sufficiently touched and affected by the awareness of his lowly state until he has compared himself with God's majesty. Moreover, we have numerous examples of this consternation both

in The Book of Judges and in the Prophets. So frequent was it that this expression was common among God's people: "We shall die, for the Lord has appeared to us" [Judg. 13:22; Isa. 6:5; Ezek. 2:1; 1:28; Judg. 6:22–23; and elsewhere].[1]

That, of course, comes from book 1 of the *Institutes*, where Calvin considers the knowledge of God *the Creator*. This dumbstruck, overwhelmed wonder is the result of considering the majesty of the Creator.

And it is right that trembling fear should be the right reaction to the Creator. It shows that the holiness of the Creator is not a quiet, anemic thing to be received with stained-glass voices and simpers. The holiness of the sovereign Lord is tremendous, vivid, and dazzling. *Not* to fear him would be blind foolishness. In fact, argued John Bunyan, those who have no fear of God are being more stupid than dumb animals, which fear humankind (Gen. 9:2). Wrote Bunyan:

> But what a shame is this to man, that God should subject all his creatures to him, and he should refuse to stoop his heart to God? The beast, the bird, the fish, and all, have a fear and dread of man, yea, God has put it in their hearts to fear man, and yet man is void of fear and dread, I mean of godly fear of him, that thus lovingly hath put all things under him. Sinner, art thou not ashamed, that a silly cow, a sheep, yea, a swine, should better observe the law of his creation, than thou dost the law of thy God?[2]

---

1   John Calvin, *Institutes of the Christian Religion*, ed. John T. McNeill, trans. Ford Lewis Battles (Louisville: Westminster John Knox, 2011), 1.1.3.

2   John Bunyan, "A Treatise on the Fear of God," in *The Works of John Bunyan*, ed. George Offer, 3 vols. (Glasgow: W. G. Blackie & Son, 1854; repr., Edinburgh: Banner of Truth, 1991), 1:478.

In the splendor of the Creator's majesty, we *should* be abased. In the brightness of his purity, we *should* be ashamed. Glimpsing his divine holiness, we should cry with Job,

> I had heard of you by the hearing of the ear,
>   but now my eye sees you;
> therefore I despise myself,
>   and repent in dust and ashes. (Job 42:5–6)

Such knowledge of the Creator produces a fear that leads to humility, repentance, and contempt for all self-complacency and self-conceit.

Fear of the Creator in Unbelievers

There is a sense in which all people, not just Christians, can know *something* of this fear of the Creator. Take, for example, Abimelech in Genesis 20, who treats Abraham's wife Sarah with respect because, though a pagan, he does have some fear of God in him (see vv. 9–11). The pantheist poet William Blake (1757–1827) poignantly expressed his fear of God in the resonant words of "The Tyger":

> Tyger Tyger, burning bright,
> In the forests of the night;
> What immortal hand or eye,
> Could frame thy fearful symmetry?
>
> In what distant deeps or skies
> Burnt the fire of thine eyes?
> On what wings dare he aspire?
> What the hand, dare seize the fire?
>
> And what shoulder, & what art,
> Could twist the sinews of thy heart?

And when thy heart began to beat,
What dread hand? & what dread feet?

What the hammer? what the chain,
In what furnace was thy brain?
What the anvil? what dread grasp,
Dare its deadly terrors clasp!

When the stars threw down their spears
And water'd heaven with their tears:
Did he smile his work to see?
Did he who made the Lamb make thee?

Tyger Tyger burning bright,
In the forests of the night:
What immortal hand or eye,
Dare frame thy fearful symmetry?[3]

What stands out here is that the fearfulness of the tiger leads Blake to consider how dreadful its Creator must be. There is something entirely right there: the Creator of such a beast must be *and is* dreadful. But Blake can see no further: he is left dreading *but not loving* the Creator. C. S. Lewis's "master," George MacDonald, wrote of this kind of fear:

The thing that is unknown, yet known to be, will always be more or less formidable. When it is known as immeasurably greater than we, and as having claims and making demands upon us, the more vaguely these are apprehended, the more room is there for anxiety; and when the conscience is not clear, this anxiety may well mount

---

3   William Blake, "The Tyger" (1794).

to terror. According to the nature of the mind which occupies itself with the idea of the Supreme, whether regarded as maker or ruler, will be the kind and degree of the terror. To this terror need belong no exalted ideas of God; those fear him most who most imagine him like their own evil selves, only beyond them in power, easily able to work his arbitrary will with them. That they hold him but a little higher than themselves, tends nowise to unity with him: who so far apart as those on the same level of hate and distrust? Power without love, dependence where is no righteousness, wake a worship without devotion, a loathliness of servile flattery.[4]

Fear of the Creator in Believers

Now compare Blake's words with those of the hymnwriter Isaac Watts as he considers the grandeur of the Creator:

Eternal power, whose high abode
Becomes the grandeur of a God,
Infinite lengths beyond the bounds
Where stars resolve their little rounds.

The lowest step around Thy seat,
Rises too high for Gabriel's feet;
In vain the tall archangel tries
To reach Thine height with wondering eyes.

Thy dazzling beauties whilst he sings,
He hides his face behind his wings,
And ranks of shining thrones around
Fall worshiping, and spread the ground.

4 George MacDonald, *Unspoken Sermons, Second Series* (London: Longmans, Green & Co., 1885), 73.

Lord, what shall earth and ashes do?
We would adore our maker, too;
From sin and dust to Thee we cry,
The Great, the Holy, and the High!

Earth from afar has heard Thy fame,
And worms have learned to lisp Thy name;
But, O! the glories of Thy mind
Leave all our soaring thoughts behind.

God is in Heaven, and men below;
Be short our tunes, our words be few;
A sacred reverence checks our songs,
And praise sits silent on our tongues.[5]

As with Blake, there is mute and dazzled wondering here. Watts feels that he is sin and dust before God's high majesty. But the tone is entirely different: Watts is full of adoration. His fear is a worshipful and devoted fear, a loving fear that falls down facing, not fleeing God.

What makes for the difference between the two poets? Very simply, Watts had been taken further in his knowledge of God. Not only did he have the knowledge of God the Creator; he also had the knowledge of God the Redeemer in Christ. And that knowledge of God as a humble, gracious, and compassionate Redeemer beautifies the sight of his transcendent majesty as Creator. Our wonder at the Creator's magnificence—and our enjoyment of it—increases when we know it as the perfect magnificence of the kindest Savior. When we know God as Redeemer, we are freed from all Blake's doubts about

---

5 Isaac Watts, "Eternal Power, Whose High Abode" (1706).

God's character, and we are freed from all fears that this awesome God might be against us. We are freed, in other words, fully to enjoy him as Creator.

Jonathan Edwards explained this Blakean "knowledge of the creator without knowledge of him as redeemer" like this:

> 'Tis possible that those who are wholly without grace, should have a clear sight, and very great and affecting sense of God's greatness, his mighty power, and awful majesty; for this is what the devils have, though they have lost the spiritual knowledge of God, consisting in a sense of the amiableness of his moral perfections; they are perfectly destitute of any sense or relish of that kind of beauty, yet they have a very great knowledge of the natural glory of God (if I may so speak) or his awful greatness and majesty; this they behold, and are affected with the apprehensions of, and therefore tremble before him.[6]

And this was very much the story Edwards told of himself in his "Personal Narrative." As a child, he wrote, his mind had been "full of objections against the doctrine of God's sovereignty."[7] Unable to rest on God, he found the knowledge of a Creator to be terrible. This came out in a particular fear of thunderstorms: "I used to be a person uncommonly terrified with thunder: and it used to strike me with terror, when I saw a thunderstorm rising."[8] Then, through reading Scripture, he began to sense the excellency of God, feeling

---

6 Jonathan Edwards, *Religious Affections*, ed. John E. Smith, vol. 2 of *The Works of Jonathan Edwards* (New Haven, CT: Yale University Press, 1959), 263.

7 Jonathan Edwards, "Personal Narrative," in *Letters and Personal Writings*, ed. George S. Claghorn, vol. 16 of *The Works of Jonathan Edwards* (New Haven, CT: Yale University Press, 1998), 791–92.

8 Edwards, "Personal Narrative," 794.

"how happy I should be, if I might enjoy that God, and be wrapt up to God in heaven."[9]

> From about that time, I began to have a new kind of apprehensions and ideas of Christ, and the work of redemption, and the glorious way of salvation by him. I had an inward, sweet sense of these things, that at times came into my heart; and my soul was led away in pleasant views and contemplations of them. And my mind was greatly engaged, to spend my time in reading and meditating on Christ; and the beauty and excellency of his person, and the lovely way of salvation, by free grace in him.[10]

Those happy thoughts of God the Redeemer in Christ entirely changed how he saw God the Creator, and transformed how he then experienced this God's glory in creation. Where once nothing had been so terrible to him as a thunderstorm,

> now, on the contrary, it rejoiced me. I felt God at the first appearance of a thunderstorm. And used to take the opportunity at such times, to fix myself to view the clouds, and see the lightnings play, and hear the majestic and awful voice of God's thunder: which often times was exceeding entertaining, leading me to sweet contemplations of my great and glorious God.[11]

Edwards's experience of the creation was different because his knowledge of the Creator had been infused with the knowledge that the high and holy one is the most gracious Redeemer. It meant that as he looked around creation, he saw it not only as the work of the

9 Edwards, "Personal Narrative," 792.
10 Edwards, "Personal Narrative," 793.
11 Edwards, "Personal Narrative," 794.

Creator but as the work of the one who was both his Creator *and* his Redeemer. And so, as he

> looked up on the sky and clouds; there came into my mind, a sweet sense of the glorious majesty and grace of God, that I know not how to express. I seemed to see them both in a sweet conjunction: majesty and meekness joined together: it was a sweet and gentle, and holy majesty; and also a majestic meekness; an awful sweetness; a high, and great, and holy gentleness.
>
> After this my sense of divine things gradually increased, and became more and more lively, and had more of that inward sweetness. The appearance of everything was altered: there seemed to be, as it were, a calm, sweet cast, or appearance of divine glory, in almost everything. God's excellency, his wisdom, his purity and love, seemed to appear in everything; in the sun, moon and stars; in the clouds, and blue sky; in the grass, flowers, trees; in the water, and all nature; which used greatly to fix my mind. I often used to sit and view the moon, for a long time; and so in the daytime, spent much time in viewing the clouds and sky, to behold the sweet glory of God in these things: in the meantime, singing forth with a low voice, my contemplations of the Creator and Redeemer.[12]

Charles Spurgeon argued that while believers have an adoring fear of God, "we, who believe in Jesus, are not afraid of God even as our King."[13] For we know the beautiful *character* of the one who rules: the sovereign Creator is a gracious and merciful Redeemer. Those who are taught only—or even predominantly—that God is King

---

12 Edwards, "Personal Narrative," 793–94.
13 C. H. Spurgeon, "A Fear to Be Desired," in *The Metropolitan Tabernacle Pulpit Sermons*, 63 vols. (London: Passmore & Alabaster, 1855–1917), 48:498.

and Creator will be left with William Blake's dread. Only those who also get to hear of God's redeeming graciousness to sinners will begin to share Edwards's pleasure in his Creator. Or Spurgeon's, for that matter. Hear how similar he sounds:

> Gazing upon the vast expanse of waters,—looking up to the innumerable stars, examining the wing of an insect, and seeing there the matchless skill of God displayed in the minute; or standing in a thunderstorm, watching, as best you can, the flashes of lightning, and listening to the thunder of Jehovah's voice, have you not often shrunk into yourself, and said, "Great God, how terrible art thou!"—not afraid, but full of delight, like a child who rejoices to see his father's wealth, his father's wisdom, his father's power,—happy, and at home, but feeling oh, so little![14]

Spurgeon was quakingly delighted (and not afraid) because the immensity of the heavens and the complexity of the insects and the might of the thunder all came from "his *father's* wealth, his *father's* wisdom, his *father's* power." He knew the Creator was his Father in Christ.

The Benefits of This Fear

Safe in the knowledge that the awesome Creator is our tender Redeemer, Christians can delight themselves in the overwhelming majesty of the Creator. In fact, contemplating the splendor of God and so stoking our fearful wonder at him is at the heart of Christian health. "And we all, with unveiled face, *beholding the glory of the Lord,* are being transformed into the same image from one degree of glory

14 Spurgeon, "A Fear to Be Desired," 496.

to another" (2 Cor. 3:18). The grandeur of God pulls our focus up and away from ourselves. We wonder at a being greater than us. We therefore diminish. His magnificence distracts us and woos us from our daily self-obsession. We develop a taste for something other than ourselves. At the same time, our thoughts are lifted and cleansed as we consider one who is greater and purer than us.

The tragedy here is that such knowledge of God for its own sake is commonly treated *by Christians* as a cerebral and impractical luxury. We like books that show us "how to . . ."; we like sermons that give us something to do. They feel more productive. And that's not wrong. But "*this* is eternal life, that they know you, the only true God, and Jesus Christ whom you have sent" (John 17:3). Amid our hectic lives, amid all our challenges and trials, it is the fresh contemplation of the glory of God that will bring the right, bigger, healthier, happier perspective to all we are going through.

The great Puritan theologian John Owen knew this well from personal experience. Owen was a man painfully familiar with heartbreak. In the second half of his life, not only was he hampered in ministry and harassed by the government; he also had to witness the burial of all eleven of his children, as well as his wife, Mary. Yet, after the death of the first ten children, he wrote these words:

> A due contemplation of the glory of Christ will restore and compose the mind. . . . [It] will lift the minds and hearts of believers above all the troubles of this life, and is the sovereign antidote that will expel all the poison that is in them; which otherwise might perplex and enslave their souls.[15]

---

15 John Owen, *The Glory of Christ*, vol. 1 of *The Works of John Owen*, ed. William H. Goold (repr., Edinburgh: Banner of Truth, 1965), 279.

Fresh contemplation of the glory of God not only lifts and brightens our perspective; it also is precisely what enlivens. As Owen went on to say:

> Do any of us find decays in grace prevailing in us;—deadness, coldness, lukewarmness, a kind of spiritual stupidity and senselessness coming upon us? . . . Let us assure ourselves there is no better way for our healing and deliverance, yea, no other way but this alone,—namely, the obtaining a fresh view of the glory of Christ by faith, and a steady abiding therein. Constant contemplation of Christ and his glory, putting forth its transforming power unto the revival of all grace, is the only relief in this case.[16]

Recent scientific studies confirm some of these benefits of awe for healthy living. In 2018, the *Journal of Personality and Social Psychology* reported on a series of studies that sought to show how experiences of awe promote greater humility. They found that "when individuals encounter an entity that is vast and challenges their worldview, they feel awe, which leads to self-diminishment and subsequently humility." They also found that "inducing awe led participants to present a more balanced view of their strengths and weaknesses to others . . . and acknowledge, to a greater degree, the contribution of outside forces in their own personal accomplishments."[17]

Another set of studies published in 2018, in *Emotion*, sought to demonstrate the impact of awe on well-being and stress-related symptoms. The authors found that for every participant in the studies, after experiences of awe, symptoms of post-traumatic stress disorder

---

16 Owen, *The Glory of Christ*, 395.

17 J. E. Stellar et al., "Awe and Humility," *Journal of Personality and Social Psychology* 114, no. 2 (2018): 258–69, quoting 258.

decreased, while scores of general happiness, satisfaction with life, and social well-being, all improved.[18] This followed a report in the same journal in 2015 showing that people who experienced more awe also appeared to have better immune health. Studying the effect of emotions on pro-inflammatory cytokines (high levels of which have been associated with conditions like diabetes, heart disease, and depression), researchers found that awe was the emotion most likely linked to lower levels of these molecules.[19]

The Idea of the Holy

Almost certainly the best-known and most influential study of this fear of the Creator is that of the German liberal theologian Rudolf Otto. In his 1917 work *Das Heilige* (*The Idea of the Holy*), Otto coined the term "numinous," from the Latin *numen* ("spirit" or "divinity," originally referring to a divine or spiritual being). The numinous, he argued, is the quintessential religious experience that is beyond our reason. It is the experience of something "wholly other," something he called a *mysterium tremendum et fascinans*. By that he meant that the numinous is (1) mysterious and inexpressible, (2) tremendous or awe-inspiring, and (3) fascinating. The numinous is beautiful and terrible, fascinating and daunting, alluring and overwhelming—all at the same time. Otto described the *mysterium tremendum* like this:

> The feeling of it may at times come sweeping like a gentle tide, pervading the mind with a tranquil mood of deepest worship. It may pass over into a more set and lasting attitude of the soul,

---

18 C. L. Anderson, M. Monroy, and D. Keltner, "Awe in Nature Heals: Evidence from Military Veterans, At-Risk Youth, and College Students," *Emotion* 18, no. 8 (2018): 1195–1202.

19 J. E. Stellar et al., "Positive Affect and Markers of Inflammation: Discrete Positive Emotions Predict Lower Levels of Inflammatory Cytokines," *Emotion* 15, no. 2 (2015): 129–33.

continuing, as it were, thrillingly vibrant and resonant, until at last it dies away and the soul resumes its "profane," non-religious mood of everyday experience. It may burst in sudden eruption up from the depths of the soul with spasms and convulsions, or lead to the strangest excitements, to intoxicated frenzy, to transport, and to ecstasy. It has its wild and daemonic forms and can sink to an almost grisly horror and shuddering. And again it may be developed into something beautiful and pure and glorious. It may become the hushed, trembling, and speechless humility of the creature in the presence of—whom or what? In the presence of that which is a *mystery* inexpressible and above all creatures.[20]

Otto's argument has been hugely influential in the English-speaking world. C. S. Lewis, for example, listed *The Idea of the Holy* among the ten books that most shaped his vocational attitude and philosophy of life.[21] And you don't need to be a Lewis scholar to see how deeply Otto shaped Lewis. You can feel the numinous in the very air of Narnia, especially in the presence of Aslan. Think, for example, of the first time Mr. Beaver mentions Aslan's name in *The Lion, the Witch and the Wardrobe*:

"They say Aslan is on the move—perhaps he has already landed."

And now a very curious thing happened. None of the children knew who Aslan was any more than you do; but the moment Beaver had spoken these words everyone felt quite different. Perhaps it has sometimes happened to you in a dream that someone says something which you don't understand but in the dream it feels as if it had some enormous meaning—either a terrifying one which

20 Rudolph Otto, *The Idea of the Holy* (New York: Oxford University Press, 1958), 12–13.
21 C. S. Lewis, "Ex Libris," *The Christian Century* 79 (June 6, 1962): 719.

turns the whole dream into a nightmare or else a lovely meaning too lovely to put into words, which makes the dream so beautiful that you remember it all your life and are always wishing you could get into the dream again. It was like that now. At the name of Aslan each one of the children felt something jump in its inside. Edmund felt a sensation of mysterious horror. Peter felt suddenly brave and adventurous. Susan felt as if some delicious smell or some delightful strain of music had just floated by her. And Lucy got the feeling you have when you wake up in the morning and realize that it is the beginning of the holidays or the beginning of summer.[22]

Kenneth Grahame captured the same experience in fiction for children to understand in *The Wind in the Willows*. There, Rat and Mole go to see if they can find "The Piper at the Gates of Dawn" (the god Pan, pagan deity of nature and the wild). What they get is a truly epiphanic, "numinous" experience.

Then suddenly the Mole felt a great Awe fall upon him, an awe that turned his muscles to water, bowed his head, and rooted his feet to the ground. It was no panic terror—indeed he felt wonderfully at peace and happy—but it was an awe that smote and held him and, without seeing, he knew it could only mean that some august Presence was very, very near. With difficulty he turned to look for his friend and saw him at his side cowed, stricken, and trembling violently. And still there was utter silence in the populous bird-haunted branches around them; and still the light grew and grew.

Perhaps he would never have dared to raise his eyes, but that, though the piping was now hushed, the call and the summons

---

22 C. S. Lewis, *The Lion, the Witch and the Wardrobe* (London: Geoffrey Bles, 1950), 65.

seemed still dominant and imperious. He might not refuse, were Death himself waiting to strike him instantly, once he had looked with mortal eye on things rightly kept hidden. Trembling he obeyed, and raised his humble head; and then, in that utter clearness of the imminent dawn, while Nature, flushed with fulness of incredible colour, seemed to hold her breath for the event, he looked in the very eyes of the Friend and Helper . . . and still, as he looked, he lived; and still, as he lived, he wondered.

"Rat!" he found breath to whisper, shaking. "Are you afraid?"

"Afraid?" murmured the Rat, his eyes shining with unutterable love. "Afraid! Of Him? O, never, never! And yet—and yet—O, Mole, I am afraid!"

Then the two animals, crouching to the earth, bowed their heads and did worship.[23]

Otto (and Lewis and Grahame) managed to capture very well something about the fear of the Creator. As we have seen, the Creator *is* the definitive *mysterium tremendum et fascinans*. He is inexpressibly tremendous and fascinating. He is a majestic, consuming fire whose splendor causes dread in sinners and delight in saints. However, we need to be careful with Otto's argument and not imagine that it manages to capture a complete and rounded biblical portrayal of the right fear of God.

Otto was profoundly influenced and his thought molded at the deepest level by the man known as the father of modern liberal theology, Friedrich Schleiermacher (1768–1834). Schleiermacher held that all religions are simply different expressions of the same universal religious instinct or feeling. Some religions (like Christianity) are

---

23 K. Grahame, *The Wind in the Willows* (London: Methuen & Co., 1908), 133–36.

simply more evolved than others, he taught. Otto was prepared to be critical of Schleiermacher in places, but at this point he simply toed the party line, teaching that Christianity is superior to other religions not "as truth is superior to falsehood but as Plato is superior to Aristotle."[24] Thus, when Otto came to describe the numinous, *he never pretended he was attempting to describe a specifically Christian idea* (just as, when we read of Rat and Mole's encounter with Pan, it is not clear whether Grahame is depicting a pagan or a Christian experience). It was something Otto saw in many religions, from primitive paganism to modern Buddhism. In other words, while Otto managed to describe something akin to the knowledge of the Creator, he was *not* describing the knowledge of God the Redeemer in Christ. His description of the *mysterium tremendum*, then, cannot tell us about that uniquely and specifically Christian fear: the fear of God the Redeemer in Christ.

Given the brilliance, genuine wisdom, and wide influence of *The Idea of the Holy*, it would be easy to take Otto's description of the *mysterium tremendum* as a complete map for what Scripture calls "the fear of God." But it was never intended to be. And three main problems arise if we do.

First, Otto focuses almost exclusively on our relationship to God as a creature-Creator relationship. The numinous, he argues, is associated primarily with "creature-feeling" and secondarily with overpowering might. He therefore has no strong conception of redemption or of the gracious *character* of the Creator who wields that overpowering might. To put it bluntly, Otto's "wholly other" is lacking in much loveable personality. In fairness to Otto, he describes the numinous

---

24 Rudolf Otto, *Religious Essays: A Supplement to "The Idea of the Holy,"* trans. Brian Lunn (London: Oxford University Press, 1931), 114.

as fascinating and sees something of the longing and yearning involved in right fear, but he is unable to account for it well. To see the deficiency properly, contrast it with a conception of God that is highly aware of God as gracious Redeemer, as in Jonathan Edwards's description of God in his holiness.

> God is arrayed with an infinite brightness, a brightness that doesn't create pain as the light of the sun pains the eyes to behold it, but rather fills with excess of joy and delight. Indeed, no man can see God and live, because the sight of such glory would overpower nature, . . .'tis because the joy and pleasure in beholding would be too strong for a frail nature.[25]

According to Edwards, God is dazzling in his holiness and overwhelmingly fascinating—but not simply because of his overpowering might. Knowing the almighty Creator as a glorious Redeemer enables Edwards to see deeper than Otto into the nature of God's holiness. Edwards sees that, above all God's omnipotence, he is dazzling *in the superfluence and superabundance of his very being and blessedness.*

Second, this all means that Otto's understanding of the fear of God is essentially limited to the fear of the Creator. Otto shows little evidence of seriously grasping that there might be a higher fear than that of the creature before its Creator. When, for example, he describes the fear of the patriarchs, he conceives it solely as their consciousness of their own creaturehood in the presence of deity. It was "the emotion of a creature, submerged and overwhelmed by its own nothingness

---

25 Jonathan Edwards, "That God Is the Father of Lights," in *The Blessing of God: Previously Unpublished Sermons of Jonathan Edwards*, ed. M. McMullen (Nashville: Broadman & Holman, 2003), 346.

in contrast to that which is supreme above all creatures."[26] But, as we have seen, that is not a conclusion drawn from the text of Genesis: the context of Jacob's fear at Bethel is the catalog of the Lord's blessings overwhelming him with goodness. The limits of Otto's theological perspective curtailed his understanding of the fear of God: it would mean little more than awe at God's transcendence and otherness. And that shortsightedness has serious consequences. Otto argued, for example, that "the feeling of one's own submergence, of being but 'dust and ashes' and nothingness . . . forms the numinous raw material for the feeling of religious humility."[27] As with so much of what Otto says, there is truth here: the feeling of our nothingness before God's immensity *should* humble us. However, it is not the *only* facet of God's holiness that humbles us. More than God's immensity, the humility and grace of the Redeemer—seen ultimately in the cross—fuel a deeper and more eager humility in believers.

Third, Otto's idea of the *mysterium tremendum, left to itself,* all too easily collapses into simply being afraid of God. It is ironic that Otto was a Lutheran, for this was something Martin Luther foresaw when he wrote: "We were totally unable to come to a recognition of the Father's favor and grace except through the Lord Christ, who is the mirroring image of the Father's heart. Without Christ we see nothing in God but an angry and terrible Judge."[28] Not having come to his knowledge of the *mysterium tremendum* through Christ, Otto is left with a God who is only other or against us. Thus for him it must primarily and overwhelmingly be God's transcendence and wrath that elicit our awe. Indeed, wrote Otto, "ὀργή [*orgē*, God's wrath] is

---

26 Otto, *The Idea of the Holy*, 10.
27 Otto, *The Idea of the Holy*, 20.
28 *Luther's Large Catechism* (St. Louis, MO: Concordia, 1978), 77.

nothing but the *tremendum* itself."[29] At this, we need to hear Professor John Murray's helpful wisdom:

> The fear of God which is the soul of godliness does not consist, however, in the dread which is produced by the apprehension of God's wrath. When the reason for such dread exists, then to be destitute of it is the sign of hardened ungodliness. But the fear of God which is the basis of godliness, and in which godliness may be said to consist, is much more inclusive and determinative than the fear of God's judgement. And we must remember that the dread of judgement will never of itself generate within us the love of God or hatred of the sin that makes us liable to his wrath. Even the infliction of wrath will not create the hatred of sin; it will incite to greater love of sin and enmity against God. Punishment has of itself no regenerating or converting power. The fear of God in which godliness consists is the fear which constrains adoration and love.[30]

Different Gods, Different Fears

Part of the problem with Otto's account is that he was looking only for *common* or *shared* experiences of the numinous across different religions. What defines the numinous, after all, is simply an experience of a spiritual—instead of a physical—reality. By definition it is an experience of something "other," but no more defined than that. However, while there clearly are common numinous experiences across different religions, there are also important differences.

Fear first made gods in the world, said the ancient Romans. But each different god then induced a different *sort* of fear, for the nature

---

29 Otto, *The Idea of the Holy*, 18.
30 John Murray, *Principles of Conduct: Aspects of Biblical Ethics* (London: Tyndale, 1957), 236.

and character of each god shaped the nature and character of the fear it induced. In Greco-Roman paganism, the gods were feared in only a vague way. They were simply not magnificent enough to command more. True, Zeus was said to have a beauty and radiance that was almost painful to behold. But generally they were more flattered than feared—and if they were feared, it was for their fickle capriciousness and petty vindictiveness. In Hinduism, the severed-head-wielding goddess of destruction, Kali, is feared in a way quite different than the more benign Krishna. And in Islam, *taqwa* (the fear of Allah) is a concept that, first of all, has implied external dutifulness and faithful observance, not a quaking internal state of heart. After that, *taqwa* has come to include a more internal emotional state: the fear of Allah's punishment. In each case, the nature of the god in question shapes the appropriate fear response.

Given these differences, Christians need to press beyond the fact that the living God is the Creator to know what sort of being God is in himself. Knowing God the Redeemer in Christ will make our Christian fear distinct from the fear shown by the devotees of other gods. It is what we need if our fear is to be specifically and happily *Christian*.

5

Overwhelmed by the Father

WHAT WAS GOD DOING before creation? That was a question at the heart of a debate that raged through the fourth century AD. People wanted to know what God was like *in himself*, in the privacy of eternity, before he ever ruled creation or had any dealings with his creatures. It all started in Egypt when an Alexandrian elder named Arius began teaching that the Son was a created being and not truly God. Arius taught this because he believed that God is the origin and cause of everything but is not caused to exist by anything else. "Uncaused" or "Unoriginate," he therefore held, was the best and most basic definition of what God is like. And, he argued, since the Son, being a son, must have received his being from the Father, he could not, by definition, be God.

The Father Revealed in the Son

Believing that Arius had started in the wrong place with his basic definition of God, Arius's young contemporary Athanasius responded with an assertion so important it would echo through the centuries: "It is more pious and more accurate to signify God from the Son and call Him Father, than to name Him from His works only and call

Him Unoriginate."[1] In other words, the right way to think about God is not to think of him primarily as Creator (naming him "from His works only"). For if God's essential identity is to be the Creator, the ruler, then he needs a creation to rule *in order to be who he is*. But God existed for eternity before he ever created, and he existed with complete self-sufficiency, depending on nothing to be who he is. He is not a God who needs anything (Acts 17:25). He has life in himself (John 5:26). He is *a se* (from himself). And that being the case, argued Athanasius, we cannot come to a true knowledge of who God is in himself simply by looking at him as Creator. We must listen to how he has revealed himself—and he has revealed himself in his Son, making known that revelation in all the Scriptures. Our most basic definition of who God is flows from the Son who reveals him. And when we start with the Son and his word, we find that the first (though not only) thing to say about God is, as the Nicene Creed begins, "We believe in one God, *the Father*." Through the Son we see behind creation into the eternal and essential identity of God. It is as if, through Christ, we step inside the front door of God's home to see who he is behind what he does.

The same concerns resurfaced in the Reformation. The Reformers saw how easily we can speak of God "from His works only" without reference to his self-revelation. They therefore applied the principle of *sola Scriptura* to the doctrine of God, arguing that God is known truly not through the unaided efforts of fallen human minds but through the preaching of Christ in the gospel. So, wrote Philipp Melanchthon, "We seek a God who has revealed himself." And how? Christ, he explained,

---

1 Athanasius, *Against the Arians*, 1.34, in *A Select Library of Nicene and Post-Nicene Fathers of the Christian Church*, ser. 2, ed. Philip Schaff and Henry Wace, 14 vols. (1886–1889; repr. Peabody, MA: Hendrickson, 1994), 4:326.

leads us to the revealed God in this way. When Philip begged that the Father be shown to them, John 14:8–9, the Lord earnestly rebuked him and said, "He who has seen Me has seen the Father." He did not wish God to be sought by idle and vagrant speculations, but He wills that our eyes be fixed on the Son who has been manifested to us, that our prayers be directed to the eternal Father who has revealed himself in the Son whom he has sent.[2]

The deepest revelation of God's glory and nature is found in his identity as Redeemer. Consider, for example, how Isaiah speaks of "the Holy One of Israel." The Holy One, high and lifted up, incomparable in his power and purity, is "the God of the whole earth" (54:5). He is the Maker who "laid the foundation of the earth" (48:13). He created man (41:4; 43:1; 54:5) and commands nature (41:18–19; 43:20; 49:11). Yet, in each of these passages, Isaiah speaks of the Holy One *as* the "Redeemer" (41:14; 43:14; 47:4; 48:17; 49:7).

> For your Maker is your husband,
>> the LORD of hosts is his name;
> and the Holy One of Israel is your Redeemer. (54:5)

Indeed, cries Isaiah,

> you are our Father, . . .
> you, O LORD, are our Father,
>> our Redeemer from of old is your name. (63:16)

Therefore the deepest reality of what it means for him to be "high and lifted up" (6:1) is unfolded only when the suffering servant is

---

2 Philipp Melanchthon, *Loci Communes* (1543), trans. J. A. O. Preus (St. Louis, MO: Concordia, 1992), 18.

"high and lifted up" (52:13). Most supremely, it is in that moment that "the glory of the LORD shall be revealed" (40:5). Jesus himself would go on to speak of the cross as "the hour" of his glorification, when he would be "lifted up from the earth" (John 12:23, 32). John Calvin concluded, "In all the creatures, indeed, both high and low, the glory of God shines, but nowhere has it shone more brightly than in the cross."[3]

With this in mind Calvin divided our knowledge of God into two steps or levels: the knowledge of God the Creator (*Institutes*, book 1), and the knowledge of God the Redeemer in Christ (*Institutes*, book 2). But to be clear, Calvin did not think it acceptable—or possible—for Christians to stop with the knowledge of God the Creator only. Those who think of God as *only* Creator are "lost and accursed," he argued. "For until men recognize that they owe everything to God, that they are nourished by his fatherly care, that he is the Author of their every good, that they should seek nothing beyond him—they will never yield him willing service."[4] Indeed, that is precisely our problem as sinners in a fallen world, that in "this ruin of mankind no one now experiences God either as Father or as Author of salvation, or favorable in any way, until Christ the Mediator comes forward to reconcile him to us."[5] Calvin wanted Christians to think of the almighty Creator as their Father. Indeed, we do not truly understand God's work as Creator or his providence (and so we have no comfort) unless we understand that it is a *fatherly* work. Calvin held that "we ought in the very order of things [in creation] diligently to contemplate God's

---

3 John Calvin, *Commentary on the Gospel according to John*, vol. 2, in *Calvin's Commentaries*, trans. William Pringle (Grand Rapids, MI: Baker, 1989), at John 13:31.

4 John Calvin, *Institutes of the Christian Religion*, ed. John T. McNeill, trans. Ford Lewis Battles (Louisville: Westminster John Knox, 2011), 1.2.1.

5 Calvin, *Institutes*, 1.2.1.

fatherly love."[6] He wrote, "To conclude once for all, whenever we call God the Creator of heaven and earth, let us at the same time bear in mind that . . . we are indeed his children, whom he has received into his faithful protection to nourish and educate."[7]

Moreover, Calvin wanted to draw his readers on to know of the Son returning us "to God our Author and Maker, from whom we have been estranged, in order that he may again begin to be our Father."[8] For without that knowledge of the Son as our Redeemer and the Father as *our* Father in Christ, we simply do not properly know God. And, Calvin would go on, it is the work of the Spirit precisely to give us that certain knowledge. He argued that the first title of the Spirit is the

> "spirit of adoption" because he is the witness to us of the free benevolence of God with which God the Father has embraced us in his beloved only-begotten Son to become a Father to us; and he encourages us to have trust in prayer. In fact, he supplies the very words so that we may fearlessly cry, "Abba, Father!" [Rom. 8:15; Gal. 4:6].[9]

Filial Fear

"The fear of the LORD is the beginning of knowledge" (Prov. 1:7), and that deeper knowledge of God—through Christ—must lead to a deeper, richer *and sweeter* fear. It leads us from knowing God as the Creator to knowing him as our Redeemer and our Father. It is not that we will ever stop knowing him as the transcendent Creator; rather

6 Calvin, *Institutes*, 1.14.2.
7 Calvin, *Institutes*, 1.14.22.
8 Calvin, *Institutes*, 2.6.1.
9 Calvin, *Institutes*, 3.1.3.

the knowledge that he is our Father makes his creative awesomeness purely wonderful to us. By opening our eyes to know God aright, the Spirit turns our hearts to fear him aright—with a loving, *filial* fear.

George Offor, who wrote a foreword to John Bunyan's "Treatise on the Fear of God," described Bunyan's "great line of distinction" that defines right Christian fear of God:

> The great line of distinction that Bunyan draws is between that terror and dread of God, as the infinitely Holy One, before whom all sin must incur the intensity of punishment; and the love of God, as the Father of mercies, and fountain of blessedness, in the gift of his Son, and a sense of adoption into his family; by the influences of which the soul fears to offend him. This fear is purely evangelical; for if the slightest dependence is placed upon any supposed good works of our own, the filial fear of God is swallowed up in dread and terror.[10]

That is the "evangelical" fear that is appropriate for Christians, who are brought by the Son not merely to be accepted creatures before the great Judge but also to be beloved, adopted, and adoring children before their heavenly Father.

Martin Luther knew well how much Christ's redemption and the fatherhood of God changes how we fear God. From his earliest days, Luther had feared God with a loveless dread. As a monk, his mind was filled with the knowledge that God is righteous and hates sin; but Luther failed to see any further into who God is—what his righteousness is and *why* he hates sin. As a result, he said, "I did not

---

10 George Offor, "Advertisement by the Editor," in John Bunyan, "A Treatise on the Fear of God," in *The Works of John Bunyan*, ed. George Offer, 3 vols. (Glasgow: W. G. Blackie & Son, 1854; repr., Edinburgh: Banner of Truth, 1991), 1:437.

love, yes, I hated the righteous God who punishes sinners, and secretly, if not blasphemously, certainly murmuring greatly, I was angry with God."[11] Not knowing God as a kind and compassionate Father, a God who brings us close, Luther found he could not love him. He and his fellow monks transferred their affections to Mary and various other saints, whom they would love and to whom they would pray.

That changed when Luther began to see that God is a fatherly God who shares, who gives to us his righteousness, and shares with us his blessedness. Looking back later in life, Luther reflected that, as a monk, he had not actually been worshiping the right God, for it is "not enough," he then said, to know God as the Creator and Judge. Only when God is known as a loving Father is he known aright. "For although the whole world has most carefully sought to understand the nature, mind and activity of God, it has had no success in this whatever. But . . . God Himself has revealed and disclosed the deepest profundity of his fatherly heart, His sheer inexpressible love."[12] Our natural problem as sinners, Luther explained, is that "we were totally unable to come to a recognition of the Father's favor and grace except through the Lord Christ, who is the mirroring image of the Father's heart. Without Christ we see nothing in God but an angry and terrible Judge."[13]

Through sending his Son to bring us back to himself, God has revealed himself to be inexpressibly loving and supremely fatherly. Luther found that not only does that give great assurance and joy—it also wins our hearts to him, for "we may look into His fatherly

---

11 Martin Luther, "Preface to the Complete Edition of Luther's Latin Writings, 1545," in *Luther's Works*, vol. 34, *Career of the Reformer IV*, ed. Jaroslav Jan Pelikan, Hilton C. Oswald, and Helmut T. Lehmann (St. Louis, MO: Concordia, 1999), 336–37.

12 *Luther's Large Catechism* (St. Louis, MO: Concordia, 1978), 77.

13 *Luther's Large Catechism*, 77.

heart and sense how boundlessly He loves us. That would warm our hearts, setting them aglow with thankfulness."[14] In the salvation of this God we see a God we can wholeheartedly love. Through his redemption our fear is transformed from trembling, slavish terror to trembling, filial wonder.

It is worth mentioning Luther as we come to grips with filial fear because we need a robust understanding of justification by faith alone if we are to enjoy it. For while the distinction between servile fear and filial fear is an old and venerable one, people mean rather different things by them. One example is Thomas Aquinas, that bastion of a Roman Catholic understanding of justification as a process of improvement in righteousness rather than a decisive act of God whereby the sinner is declared righteous by status in Christ. In his *Summa theologiae*, Aquinas made a distinction between types of fear but defined them as follows: "There are two sorts of fear of God: (a) *filial* fear, by which one fears offending God or being separated from Him, and (b) *servile* fear, by which one fears punishment."[15]

According to Aquinas, then, filial fear includes the fear of losing our salvation and being separated from God by our sins. But that is not how the Reformers saw it. We have just seen how George Offor put it in summarizing Bunyan: "If the slightest dependence is placed upon any supposed good works of our own, the filial fear of God is swallowed up in dread and terror."[16] Nor is Aquinas's filial fear how the Redeemer himself spoke. Jesus said, "This is the will

---

14 *Luther's Large Catechism*, 70.

15 *Summa theologiae*, II-II.19.10, in *New English Translation of St. Thomas Aquinas's "Summa Theologiae,"* trans. Alfred J. Freddoso, accessed March 4, 2020, https://www3.nd.edu/~afreddos /summa-translation/TOC-part2-2.htm.

16 Offor, "Advertisement by the Editor," 437.

of my Father, that everyone who looks on the Son and believes in him should have eternal life, and I will raise him up on the last day" (John 6:40; see also 10:28–29). The fear that is "purely evangelical" continually and wholly rests upon Christ's redemption as sufficient, not our own works. It is not left wondering if our sins might outweigh Christ's righteousness, or if Christ's righteousness needs some topping up by our own efforts. It therefore can remain constant in dependent wonder, not terror. Indeed, its wonder is only increased by the perfection of Christ's redemption and the infinity of his grace toward such extreme sinners as us.

Jesus's Own Fear

To understand aright the filial fear believers have, we must be clear that it is Jesus's own filial fear that we are brought to share. Luke's Gospel tells us that as the boy Jesus grew, he "increased in wisdom and in stature" (2:52). Yet the *fear of the Lord is the beginning of wisdom* (Prov. 9:10). Jesus could not have grown in wisdom without the fear of the Lord. And he is the Spirit-anointed Christ, who Isaiah prophesied would come forth from the stump of Jesse:

And the Spirit of the LORD shall rest upon him,
  the Spirit of wisdom and understanding,
  the Spirit of counsel and might,
  the Spirit of knowledge and the fear of the LORD.
And his delight shall be in the fear of the LORD. (Isa. 11:1–3)

God the Redeemer's great purpose in salvation was that the Son might be "the firstborn among many brothers" (Rom. 8:29), that the Son might share his sonship, bringing us with him before the one we can now enjoy as our Father. This means that not only do believers share the Son's own standing before the Father; we also share the Son's own filial delight in the fear of the Lord. Charles Spurgeon called this filial fear

> *the fear of his Fatherhood which leads us to reverence him.* When divine grace has given us the new birth, we recognize that we have entered into a fresh relationship towards God; namely, that we have become his sons and daughters. Then we realize that we have received "the Spirit of adoption, whereby we cry, Abba, Father." Now, we cannot truly cry unto God, "Abba, Father," without at the same time feeling, "Behold, what manner of love the Father hath bestowed upon us, that we should be called the sons of God." When we recognize that we are "heirs of God, and joint-heirs with Christ," children of the Highest, adopted into the family of the Eternal himself, we feel at once, as the spirit of childhood works within us, that we both love and fear our great Father in heaven, who has loved us with an everlasting love, and has "begotten us again unto a lively hope by the resurrection of Jesus Christ from the dead, to an inheritance incorruptible, and undefiled, and that fadeth not away."

Spurgeon continued:

> In this childlike fear, there is not an atom of that fear which signifies being afraid. We, who believe in Jesus, are not afraid of our Father; God forbid that we ever should be. The nearer we can get to him, the happier we are. Our highest wish is to be for ever with him, and to be lost in him; but, still, we pray that we may not grieve him; we beseech him to keep us from turning aside from him; we ask for his tender pity towards our infirmities, and plead with him to forgive us and to deal graciously with us for his dear Son's sake. As loving children, we feel a holy awe and reverence as we realize our

relationship to him who is our Father in heaven,—a dear, loving, tender, pitiful Father, yet our Heavenly Father, who "is greatly to be feared in the assembly of the saints, and to be had in reverence of all them that are about him."[17]

This filial fear is part of the Son's pleasurable adoration of his Father; indeed, it is the very emotional extremity of that wonder. It is not the dread of sinners before a holy Judge. It is not the awe of creatures before their tremendous Creator. It is the overwhelmed devotion of children marveling at the kindness and righteousness and glory and complete magnificence of the Father.

That is why it is not *at all* the same thing as being afraid of God. And that is why it was unhelpful for Aquinas to describe filial fear as the fear "by which one fears offending God or being separated from Him." Just as the Son had no need to fear for himself being separated from his Father's gracious presence (except when he hung *in our place* on the cross), so the adopted children of God need not fear in that way. If there is any fear of separation from God in believers, it is not the fear of being ultimately separated; it is the fear that our sins might part us from the warmth of enjoyed communion with God. More positively, it is the fear that inspires us to appreciate God's character and so hate sin and long to be more Christlike. Hear Spurgeon again:

> Now it would be very wrong for a child merely to restrain himself in his father's presence out of respect for him, and then break the bounds with unbridled licentiousness in his father's absence, as I fear many do. But you and I need not fall into this danger, because we are always in the presence of our heavenly Father in every

17 C. H. Spurgeon, "A Fear to Be Desired," in *The Metropolitan Tabernacle Pulpit Sermons*, 63 vols. (London: Passmore & Alabaster, 1855–1917), 48:497–98.

place. Who among us that fears God as he ought would wish to do anything anywhere which is wrong, and offensive to him. . . . A sense of the presence of God, a conscience that prompts one to say, "Thou God seest me," fosters in the soul a healthy fear which you can easily see would rather inspirit than intimidate a man. It is a filial, childlike fear, in the presence of one whom we deeply reverence, lest we should do anything contrary to his mind and will. So, then, there is a fear which arises out of a high appreciation of God's character, and a fear of the same kind which arises out of a sense of his presence. . . . Holy fear leads us to dread anything which might cause our Father's displeasure.[18]

In other words, the filial fear the Son shares with us is quite different from the sinner's dread of God and dread of punishment. It is an adoration of God that dreads sin itself, not just its punishment, for it has come to treasure God and so loathe all that is ungodly. As Calvin put it, the "pious mind" "restrains itself from sinning, not out of dread of punishment alone; but, because it loves and reveres God as Father, it worships and adores him as Lord. Even if there were no hell, it would still shudder at offending him alone."[19]

Why It Matters

Having a right knowledge of God is inextricably bound up with having a right fear of God. Those who do not know God as a merciful Redeemer and compassionate Father can never have the delight of a truly filial fear. At the very best, they can only tremble at his transcendent awesomeness as Creator. At worst, they can only shudder

18 C. H. Spurgeon, "Godly Fear and Its Goodly Consequence," in *The Metropolitan Tabernacle Pulpit Sermons*, 22:232–33.
19 Calvin, *Institutes*, 1.2.2.

at the thought that there is a righteous Judge in heaven and hate him in their hearts.

In contrast, those who know that God's holiness is not just his separateness from us sinners in his righteousness or his separateness from us creatures as Creator but also his absolute incomparability in grace, mercy, and kindness—they see the completeness of the beauty of holiness. They see the most glory, and see it truly. They see infinitely more deeply what it means that God is just and the justifier of those who have faith, that—as Jonathan Edwards put it—God's holiness does actually "consist in his love."[20] They see the glory of the cross, the glory of a loving Savior, the glory of a mighty but humble God who is not ashamed to call himself their Father. They can be amazed at a gracious Redeemer, like those who ran to Jesus in Mark's Gospel, astonished at all Jesus had done for them, astounded as if they were witnesses to a volcano (Mark 5:20; 7:37; 9:15).

It all means that—especially for those who preach and teach—we must keep a careful eye on the identity we most commonly ascribe to God. Is it lopsided in any way, ignoring something of who God has revealed himself to be? Does it, as Athanasius complained, tend to identify or name God "from His works only," or do we more accurately "signify God from the Son and call Him Father"? The question is not simply a matter of our choice of words when speaking of God. The very shape of the gospel we proclaim will speak loudest about how we most essentially think of God.

Think of the gospel presentation that describes God only as Creator and ruler or King; sin is no deeper a matter than breaking his rules;

---

20 Jonathan Edwards, "Treatise on Grace," in *Writings on the Trinity, Grace, and Faith*, ed. Sang Hyun Lee, vol. 21 of *The Works of Jonathan Edwards* (New Haven, CT: Yale University Press, 2003), 186.

redemption is solely about being brought back under his rulership. Such a gospel could never impart a *filial* fear and wonder, for there is no mention of God's fatherhood or our adoption in his Son. Such a gospel can only leave people with a fear of the Creator.

Only when we are resolutely Christ-centered—"signifying" God from the Son and so calling him Father—only then can we tell a richer, truer gospel. Only then does the story make sense that our sin is a deeper matter than external disobedience, that it is a relational matter of our hearts going astray and loving what is wrong. Only then will we speak of God the Father sending forth his Son that he might be the firstborn among many brothers, sharing his sonship and bring us as children into his family. Only that Christ-centered gospel can draw people to share Jesus's own fear.

The issue is sharpest when we touch on the question of our fear of God. When Christian teachers know the importance of the theme in Scripture but misunderstand the right fear of God as nothing but the fear of the Creator, they can actually rob believers of their filial fear. It is all too easy to point people to God's grandeur as Creator—which is absolutely right to do—but then fail to point to the gospel and God's grandeur as a compassionate Savior. A telltale sign of such truncated teaching is that it will lack the Savior's compassion and therefore come across as angry, hectoring, and unkind. God may appear great, but he will not appear good.

The two steps Calvin argues for in our knowledge of God both need to be observed if people are to fear aright: the knowledge of God the marvelous Creator *and* the knowledge of God the merciful Redeemer in Christ. And the progression from the one to the other must be maintained. For those who know God as Father can have a deeper enjoyment and fear of God as the omnipotent Creator and the righteous Judge, whereas those who know God only as Creator or Judge can never enjoy him in his redeeming loveliness. Those who know God only as Creator cannot fear him rightly as either Creator or Redeemer; only those who have a filial fear can also enjoy fearing God rightly as their Creator.

See, for example, how Charles Spurgeon's filial fear of his heavenly Father enriched his wonder at the awesomeness of God as Creator. In contrast to the unregenerate young Martin Luther, who screamed with fear at the lightning of a summer storm, Spurgeon declared, "I love the lightnings, God's thunder is my delight."

> Men are by nature afraid of the heavens; the superstitious dread the signs in the sky, and even the bravest spirit is sometimes made to tremble when the firmament is ablaze with lightning, and the pealing thunder seems to make the vast concave of heaven to tremble and to reverberate; but I always feel ashamed to keep indoors when the thunder shakes the solid earth, and the lightnings flash like arrows from the sky. Then God is abroad, and I love to walk out in some wide space, and to look up and mark the opening gates of heaven, as the lightning reveals far beyond, and enables me to gaze into the unseen. *I like to hear my Heavenly Father's voice in the thunder.*[21]

Spurgeon could relish the transcendence and creative power of God with a trembling pleasure precisely because he saw them as the transcendence and power not just of a righteous Creator but also of his loving Father. The wonders of creation are best enjoyed by the self-conscious children of God. Lightnings, mountains, stars, and wild oceans are all more marvelous to those who see them all as the works of their majestic and gracious Father.

---

21 C. H. Spurgeon, *C. H. Spurgeon's Autobiography, Compiled from His Diary, Letters, and Records, by His Wife and His Private Secretary, 1834–1854*, vol. 1 (Chicago: Curts & Jennings, 1898), 205, my emphasis.

6

How to Grow in This Fear

THIS CHAPTER'S TITLE may look like cheap self-help reader bait. How to grow in the fear of God *is* what this chapter is about, but the fear of God is not a state of mind you can guarantee with five easy steps. The fear of the Lord is wisdom (Job 28:28), but where can wisdom be found?

> It cannot be bought for gold,
>> and silver cannot be weighed as its price.
> It cannot be valued in the gold of Ophir,
>> in precious onyx or sapphire.
> Gold and glass cannot equal it,
>> nor can it be exchanged for jewels of fine gold.
> No mention shall be made of coral or of crystal;
>> the price of wisdom is above pearls.
> The topaz of Ethiopia cannot equal it,
>> nor can it be valued in pure gold.
>
> From where, then, does wisdom come?
>> And where is the place of understanding?
> It is hidden from the eyes of all living
>> and concealed from the birds of the air.

Abaddon and Death say,
> "We have heard a rumor of it with our ears."

God understands the way to it,
> and he knows its place. (Job 28:15–23)

The right fear of the Lord is a high gift, not something easily acquired. And the danger of using "how to" language is that we shift our focus from "the Fear" himself (see p. 49) to ourselves and our activities, thereby losing all possibility of genuine filial fear. We can so easily get caught up in the externals: the steps we're following or the habits we're working at. We can look at our external performance and think that our pious habits and outward displays of reverence *equal* the fear of God, when in fact we're faking it and missing the vital reality. C. S. Lewis once commented on how such external good behavior, for all its importance, is a false *ultimate* goal:

> All right, Christianity will do you good—a great deal more good than you ever wanted or expected. And the first bit of good it will do you is to hammer into your head (you won't enjoy *that!*) the fact that what you have hitherto called "good"—all that about "leading a decent life" and "being kind"—isn't quite the magnificent and all-important affair you supposed. It will teach you that in fact you can't be "good" (not for twenty-four hours) on your own moral efforts. And then it will teach you that even if you were, you still wouldn't have achieved the purpose for which you were created. Mere *morality* is not the end of life. You were made for something quite different from that. . . . Morality is indispensable: but the Divine Life, which gives itself to us and which calls us to be gods, intends for us something in which morality will be swallowed up. We are to be re-made.[1]

---

1   C. S. Lewis, "Man or Rabbit?," in *God in the Dock* (London: HarperCollins, 1979), 72.

The fear of God is the *heartbeat* of our new life in Christ and "the *soul of godliness.*"[2] As such, it is not the mere sum of certain behaviors, or something we can acquire with simple self-effort. If it were, it would be an entirely superficial and infinitely less precious matter. Instead of being a *consequence* of any particular practices, the fear of God is a matter of the deeper orientation of a renewed heart—something that *causes* truly Christian behavior.

A Matter of the Heart

The Reformers were deeply concerned with how easily we can mistake the reality of the fear of God for an outward and hollow show. As Martin Luther put it: "To fear God is not merely to fall upon your knees. Even a godless man and a robber can do that. Likewise, when a monk trusts in his cowl and rule, this is idolatry."[3] John Calvin added, "Wherever there is great ostentation in ceremonies, sincerity of heart is rare indeed."[4] That should give us pause here. It would, for example, be all too easy (and often right) to criticize church worship that seems devoid of genuine fear of God, but then as a solution simply lay down rules demanding some external performances that *mimic* true fear.

Scripture presents the fear of God as primarily an internal matter of the heart's inclinations. It describes the shape and scale of proper Christian desire. So, reads Psalm 112:1,

> Blessed is the man who fears the LORD,
>   who greatly *delights* in his commandments!

---

2 John Murray, *Principles of Conduct: Aspects of Biblical Ethics* (London: Tyndale, 1957), 229, my emphasis.

3 Martin Luther, *Luther's Works*, vol. 51, *Sermons I*, ed. Jaroslav Jan Pelikan, Hilton C. Oswald, and Helmut T. Lehmann (St. Louis, MO: Concordia, 1999), 139.

4 John Calvin, *Institutes of the Christian Religion*, ed. John T. McNeill, trans. Ford Lewis Battles (Louisville: Westminster John Knox, 2011), 1.2.2.

The one who fears the Lord, then, is not merely one who grudgingly attempts the outward action of keeping the Lord's commandments. The one who truly fears the Lord greatly delights in God's commandments!

In a brilliantly titled sermon on Proverbs 28:14, "The Happiness of Fearing Always," Thomas Boston summed up how fear is a matter of our longings—our loves and hatreds:

> Slavish fear dreads nothing but hell and punishment. Filial fear dreads sin itself. . . . The one is mixed with hatred of God, the other with love to him—the one looks on him as a revenging judge, the other as a holy father, to whose holiness the heart is reconciled and the soul longs to be conformed.[5]

In other words, fear of any sort is something that runs deeper than behavior: it is something in the very grain of the heart that *drives* behavior. Thus, sinful fear is not merely a matter of sinful actions: it *hates* God, despising him as a revenging Judge, and *therefore* acts sinfully. In contrast, a right fear *loves* God, cherishing him as a holy Father, and therefore has a sincere longing to be like him. And John Owen wrote similarly of the fear of the Lord as an internal inclination of the heart, disposing it to love him and delight in him above all: "To fear the Lord and his goodness, and to fear him for his goodness; to trust in his power and faithfulness; to obey his authority; to delight in his will and grace; to love him above all, because of his excellencies and beauty;—this is to glorify him."[6]

5 Thomas Boston, *The Whole Works of the Late Reverend Thomas Boston of Ettrick*, ed. Samuel McMillan, vol. 3 (Aberdeen: George and Robert King, 1848), 6.
6 John Owen, "An Exposition upon Psalm 130," in *Temptation and Sin*, vol. 6 of *The Works of John Owen*, ed. William H. Goold (repr., Edinburgh: Banner of Truth, 1967), 484.

The fear of God as a strong biblical theme thus stands as a superb theological guard dog. It stops us from thinking that we are made for either passionless performance or a detached knowledge of abstract truths. It backs us into the acknowledgment that we are made to know God in such a way that our hearts tremble at his beauty and splendor, that we are remade at the deepest level. It shows us that entering the life of Christ involves a transformation of our very affections, so that we begin actually to despise—and not merely renounce—the sins we once cherished, and treasure the God we once abhorred.

This is why singing is such an appropriate expression of a right, filial fear. "Clap your hands, all peoples!" cry the sons of Korah in Psalm 47;

> Shout to God with loud songs of joy!
> *For the* LORD, *the Most High, is to be feared.* (vv. 1–2; see also
>   Ps. 96:1–4)

In Exodus 15, overwhelmed by joy at the Lord's deliverance, Moses and the people *sang,*

> Who is like you, O LORD, among the gods?
>   Who is like you, majestic in holiness,
>   awesome ["fearful"] in glorious deeds, doing wonders? (v. 11)

In her Magnificat, Mary "really sings sweetly about the fear of God, what sort of Lord He is," says Luther.[7] In fact, the fear of the Lord is the reason Christianity is the most song-filled of all religions. It is the reason why, from how Christians worship together to how they stream music, they are always looking to make melody about their

---

7   Martin Luther, *Luther's Works,* vol. 21, *The Sermon on the Mount and the Magnificat,* 298.

faith. Christians instinctively want to sing to express the affection behind their words of praise, and to stir it up, knowing that words spoken flatly will not do in worship of this God. Knowing that our God rejoices over us with gladness and exults over even us with loud singing (Zeph. 3:17) makes us rejoice and exult over him in heartfelt, melodic return.

How Hearts Change

Since the fear of God is a matter of the heart's deepest inclinations, how you think you can cultivate it will depend on how you think our hearts work. And that, said Luther, was "the real issue, the essence of the matter in dispute" at the Reformation.[8]

Luther's sights in the earliest days of the Reformation were on the Aristotelian ethics that Thomas Aquinas had made so determinative for Roman Catholicism. Aristotle had claimed, "We become righteous by doing righteous deeds" (or, "we become just by doing just acts").[9] It was a self-help, fake-it-till-you-make-it message. In other words, if you work at outward righteous acts and keep doing them, you will actually become a righteous person. Aquinas therefore saw the cultivation of virtuous habits as the key to growth in holiness.

Luther's own experience as a monk had proved that wrong. For years he lived by the maxim "we become righteous by doing righteous deeds" and found, while doing all his outward acts of righteousness, it wasn't making him upright in heart, full of love for the Lord. Quite the opposite. Trying to sort himself out and become righteous by

---

8   Martin Luther, *Luther's Works*, vol. 33, *Career of the Reformer III*, 294.

9   Aristotle, *The Nicomachean Ethics*, trans. and intro. D. Ross, rev. J. L. Ackrill and J. O. Urmson (Oxford: Oxford University Press, 1998), 29.

his own efforts was driving him into a profoundly sinful fear and hatred of God. An outward *appearance* of righteousness he could achieve, but it would be nothing more than a hollow sham made of self-dependence, self-worship, and self-righteousness. Aquinas, he came to see, had failed to gauge just how deep sin goes in us, that it goes deeper down than we can ourselves reach. It is not something that can be dealt with by the behavior modification of virtuous habits. And so Luther argued in 1517, "We do *not* become righteous by doing righteous deeds but, *having been made righteous*, we do righteous deeds."[10]

As Luther saw it, our sin is not merely a matter of our actions and habits. Our actions merely manifest the deeper inclinations of our hearts: whether we love or hate God. We naturally sin because we are "carrying out the *desires* of the body" (Eph. 2:3). We choose sin because that is what we want. We naturally *love* darkness (John 3:19) and so "each person is tempted when he is lured and enticed *by his own desire.* Then desire when it has conceived gives birth to sin, and sin when it is fully grown brings forth death" (James 1:14–15).

Simply changing our habits, Luther saw, will not deal with those deeper, sinful inclinations. What we need is a *radical* renewal—not self-improvement but a profound change of heart—so that we want and love and long differently. We need hearts that freely love and are pleased with God (Ezek. 36:26–27; Mark 7:14–23; John 3:3). "How shall a work please God if it proceeds from a reluctant and resisting heart?" asked Luther.

To fulfil the law, however, is to do its works with pleasure and love. . . . This pleasure and love for the law is put into the heart

---

10 Martin Luther, *Luther's Works*, vol. 31, *Career of the Reformer I*, 12, my emphasis.

by the Holy Spirit. . . . But the Holy Spirit is not given except in, with, and by faith in Jesus Christ. . . . Faith, moreover, comes only through God's Word or gospel, which preaches Christ.[11]

That is to say, only the Holy Spirit can bring about the fundamental change in our disposition that we need, and he does this through the gospel, which preaches Christ. Only the preaching of Christ can turn a heart truly to desire righteousness and fear God with loving, trembling, filial adoration. And it is not that the Spirit does that work once only, when we are born again, leaving us from then on to sweat out our sanctification by pure self-exertion. It is *always* the gospel that does the deepest plow work in our hearts. Or, as John Owen put it, "holiness is nothing but the implanting, writing and realizing of the gospel in our souls."[12] Thus Luther's first advice for believers who desire to grow in holiness was this:

> This is how you must cultivate Christ in yourself. . . . Faith must spring up and flow from the blood and wounds and death of Christ. If you see in these that God is so kindly disposed toward you that he even gives his own Son for you, then your heart in turn must grow sweet and disposed toward God.[13]

Only then, when your heart is turned toward God, will you want to fight to turn your behavior toward him.

Today, Thomas Aquinas's language of the importance of habits has reacquired some of its old fashionable status. We need, then, to be clear what habits can and cannot do. Habits, in and of

---

11 Martin Luther, *Luther's Works*, vol. 35, *Word and Sacrament I*, 368.
12 John Owen, *The Holy Spirit*, vol. 3 of *The Works of John Owen*, ed. William H. Goold (repr., Edinburgh: Banner of Truth, 1966), 370–71.
13 Martin Luther, *Luther's Works*, vol. 44, *The Christian in Society I*, 30, 38–39.

themselves, do not have the ability to change us at the deepest level of our dispositions and desires. Rather, as Luther found, profound renewal happens from the *inside out*, with heart change driving behavior change. It cannot happen from the outside in, with behavior change working heart change. But hang on! What then, we might ask, about means of grace? What about Sunday worship? Daily devotions? Are these not virtuous habits we should cultivate? Well, not in the way Aquinas meant. The mere habit of going to church on a Sunday will not itself *necessarily* produce in us the right fear of God. Nor will reading the Bible, praying, and so on. I can maintain such habits like an unstoppable Swiss watch and still be utterly devoid of true fear of God. Those things do not convey grace *ex opere operato*. They are *means* of grace: they are points of contact with the gospel, which alone has the power to transform us. In other words, it is not the mere act of going to church that does us good; it is the gospel that we hear there. It is not the habit itself that transforms but the gospel of Christ.

This is why Moses spoke of the word of God as the means by which to cultivate a true fear of God.

> Now this is the commandment—the statutes and the rules—that the LORD your God commanded me to teach you, that you may do them in the land to which you are going over, to possess it, *that you may fear the LORD your God*, you and your son and your son's son. (Deut. 6:1–2; see also 17:18–19; 31:10–13)

As we have seen, in the middle of a string of titles describing the word of God, Psalm 19:9 calls it "the fear of the Lord," so perfectly does it reveal the glory of the one who is "the Fear." It is *through the word of God* that hearts are transformed from shaking in loathing to quaking in wonder at God.

"Were You There When They Crucified My Lord? . . . It Causes Me to Tremble"

Now, all Scripture is profitable for our growing in the filial fear of the Lord. We can look at God's wisdom in planning our salvation, his constant goodness to his people, his holiness, his greatness, his tenderness—and all these move us to know him better and so fear him more. *Everything* about him is awesome, and *all* his works proclaim how fearful he is in all his ways. Thus David prays:

> On the glorious splendor of your majesty,
>   and on your wondrous works, I will meditate.
> They shall speak of the might of your awesome ["fearful"] deeds,
>   and I will declare your greatness.
> They shall pour forth the fame of your abundant goodness
>   and shall sing aloud of your righteousness. (Ps. 145:5–7)

Scripture even tells us to look outside Scripture—to look around all creation—to see evidence of both God's magnificence and his graciousness. Thus it is when David looks at the heavens, the moon and stars, that he exclaims,

> O LORD, our Lord,
>   how majestic is your name in all the earth! (Ps. 8:9)

However, as John Calvin put it, while in "all the creatures, indeed, both high and low, the glory of God shines . . . nowhere has it shone more brightly than in the cross."[14] The cross is "the hour" when the Son of Man is glorified (John 12:23). There, "as in a magnificent

---

14 John Calvin, *Commentary on the Gospel according to John*, vol. 2, in *Calvin's Commentaries*, trans. William Pringle (Grand Rapids, MI: Baker, 1989), at John 13:31.

theatre, the inestimable goodness of God is displayed before the whole world."[15] There the fearfulness of God in all his great justice and mercy is most clearly and profoundly displayed. Thus the nineteenth-century Scottish theologian John Brown could write in his great commentary on 1 Peter:

> Nothing is so well fitted to put the fear of God, which will preserve men from offending him, into the heart, as an enlightened view of the cross of Christ. There shine spotless holiness, inflexible justice, incomprehensible wisdom, omnipotent power, holy love. None of these excellencies darken or eclipse the other, but every one of them rather gives a lustre to the rest. They mingle their beams, and shine with united eternal splendour: the just Judge, the merciful Father, the wise Governor. Nowhere does justice appear so awful, mercy so amiable, or wisdom so profound.[16]

The Puritan John Owen knew from a strong personal experience how vigorously the fear of God grows at the cross. He wrote perhaps the longest-ever exposition of Psalm 130 because of how his life was changed by verse 4 ("But with you there is forgiveness, / that you may be feared"). Owen explained:

> I myself preached Christ . . . some years, when I had but very little, if any, experimental acquaintance with access to God through Christ; until the Lord was pleased to visit me with sore affliction, whereby I was brought to the mouth of the grave, and under which my soul was oppressed with horror and darkness; but God graciously relieved my spirit by a powerful application of Psalm

---

15 Calvin, *Commentary*, John 13:31.
16 John Brown, *Expository Discourses on I Peter*, vol. 1 (Edinburgh: Banner of Truth, 1975), 472–73.

cxxx. 4, "But there is forgiveness with thee, that thou mayest be feared"; from whence I received special instruction, peace, and comfort, in drawing near to God through the Mediator, and preached thereupon immediately after my recovery.[17]

The personal significance of verse 4 to Owen is quite obvious in his commentary: it takes up about three-quarters of the work, as he spells out the nature and possibility of God's forgiveness. There Owen boldly asserts:

The fear of God, as we have showed, in the Old Testament, doth frequently express, not that gracious affection of our minds which is distinctly so called, but that whole worship of God, wherein that and all other gracious affections towards God are to be exercised. Now, the psalmist tells us that the foundation of this fear or worship, and the only motive and encouragement for sinners to engage in it and give up themselves unto it, is this, that there is forgiveness with God. Without this no sinner could fear, serve, or worship him.[18]

So why is the cross a uniquely fertile soil for the fear of God? First, because at the cross we receive the forgiveness without which we could never approach God or want to. Without Jesus's mediatorial work on the cross, God would be only a dreadful Judge to us. Preaching on Hosea 3:5 and the right fear of God, Spurgeon reasoned:

If thou fearest God, and knowest not that there is a Mediator between God and men, thou wilt never think of approaching him. God is a consuming fire, then how canst thou draw near to him

---

17 Owen, "An Exposition upon Psalm 130," 324.
18 Owen, "An Exposition upon Psalm 130," 469.

apart from Christ? If thou fearest God, and knowest not of Christ's atonement, how canst thou approach him? Without faith, it is impossible to please God, and without the blood of Jesus there is no way of access to the divine mercy-seat. If thou knowest not Christ, thou wilt never come unto God. Thy fear must link itself with the goodness of God as displayed in the person of his dear Son, or else it cannot be that seeking fear, that fear toward the Lord, of which our text speaks. It will be a fleeing fear,—a fear that will drive thee further and yet further away from God, into greater and deeper darkness,—into dire destruction,—in fact, into that pit whose bottomless abyss swallows up all hope, all rest, and all joy for ever.[19]

Spurgeon was speaking of the unbeliever who does not know Christ. But in fact too much of the same problem remains in Christians too. Though they have been enlightened by the Spirit concerning their sins, their knowledge of God's forgiveness remains patchy. And without that comfort of the gospel, they are left with a sinful dread of God, lurching between the spiritual highs of a Sunday and the spiritual sulks of a Monday, where they crawl away from God in guilt. Justification by faith alone is the essential foundation for a healthy Christian life, and ignorance of it is the very opposite of bliss. That is why Owen, in his commentary on Psalm 130, was so eager to spell out the truth of Christ's work on the cross and his justification: he saw it as the key to liberation from sinful fear. To all believers caught in such sinful fears of God, George MacDonald urged:

If then any child of the father finds that he is afraid before him, that the thought of God is a discomfort to him, or even a terror, let him

19 C. H. Spurgeon, "A Fear to Be Desired," in *The Metropolitan Tabernacle Pulpit Sermons*, 63 vols. (London: Passmore & Alabaster, 1855–1917), 48:495.

make haste—let him not linger to put on any garment, but rush at once in his nakedness, a true child, for shelter from his own evil and God's terror, into the salvation of the Father's arms, the home whence he was sent that he might learn that it was home. What father being evil would it not win to see the child with whom he was vexed running to his embrace? how much more will not the Father of our spirits, who seeks nothing but his children themselves, receive him with open arms![20]

The cross, by the forgiveness it brings, liberates us from sinful fear. But, far more than that, it also cultivates the most exquisitely fearful adoration of the Redeemer. Think of the sinful woman with Jesus at the house of Simon the Pharisee: standing at Jesus's feet, "weeping, she began to wet his feet with her tears and wiped them with the hair of her head and kissed his feet and anointed them with the ointment" (Luke 7:38). At this, Jesus said to Simon:

Do you see this woman? I entered your house; you gave me no water for my feet, but she has wet my feet with her tears and wiped them with her hair. You gave me no kiss, but from the time I came in she has not ceased to kiss my feet. You did not anoint my head with oil, but she has anointed my feet with ointment. Therefore I tell you, her sins, which are many, are forgiven—for she loved much. But he who is forgiven little, loves little. (Luke 7:44–47)

Jesus spoke of her *love*, but the intense physicality of her demonstration of affection fits Scripture's picture of *fear*. Hers was an intensely

<hr />

20 George MacDonald, *Unspoken Sermons, Second Series* (London: Longmans, Green & Co., 1885), 74.

fearful love. Or, to put it another way, her love was so intense, it was fearful. Spurgeon could have been speaking of her when he said:

> When a man really receives the pardon of all his sins, he is the man who fears the Lord. This is clearly the case, for pardon breeds *love* in the soul; and the more a man is forgiven, the more he loves. Where great sin has been blotted out, there comes to be great love. Well, is not love the very core of the true fear of God?[21]

When the awesome magnitude of Christ's forgiveness, the extent to which he has gone to atone for us, and therefore the terrible gravity of our sin become clear to us—as they do best at the cross—the right, loving reaction is so intense, it is fearful. In the same sermon, Spurgeon would go on to explain:

> There have lived, and there are living now, men and women, who have given their whole selves to Jesus, many of whom are labouring for him even beyond their strength; ay, and many such men and women have died, for his sake, the most cruel deaths, without shrinking back, or seeking to escape that terrible cross. Whence came such a fear of God as that? Why, it could never have come into their hearts if they had not received the forgiveness of their sins for Christ's sake; but, having been forgiven, they came to love and fear—not with a servile fear, but with a holy awe,—the blessed One through whose precious blood they had been cleansed. Thus, forgiveness of sin is essential to true fear of God; and wherever it is enjoyed, it is the main motive which moves them to fear God, and brings them into that blessed condition.[22]

---

21 C. H. Spurgeon, "Forgiveness and Fear," in *The Metropolitan Tabernacle Pulpit Sermons*, 50:224.
22 Spurgeon, "Forgiveness and Fear," 224.

All Christians should recognize something of this fear-filled reaction to the cross. It is an intense, wonderful, and *normal* experience for Christians. However, we also sigh at how it is too *rare* an experience. Our self-involved pride puts up its every barrier to such humiliation at the feet of Christ, even though that abasement there is so sweet. Such weak-kneed fear is a rare jewel because it is the experience of one who is willingly dying to self. George MacDonald diagnosed this wrestling with sin and experience of fear when he wrote:

> Self, accepted as the law of self, is the one demon-enemy of life; God is the only Saviour from it. . . . No glory even of God should breed terror; when a child of God is afraid, it is a sign that the word Father is not yet freely fashioned by the child's spiritual mouth. The glory can breed terror only in him who is capable of being terrified by it; while he is such it is well the terror should be bred and maintained, until the man seek refuge from it in the only place where it is not—in the bosom of the glory.[23]

All too easily we Christians settle for a sinful fear of God because we cannot handle the judgment of the cross on our sinfulness. It is when we accept that judgment and die to ourselves that our resisting dread of God turns to fearful adoration. No wonder the fear of God is a prize that cannot be bought for gold: the opposite of self-improvement, it is the fruit of a self-dying that can happen only at the foot of the cross.

We have been asking why the cross is so fertile a soil for the fear of God, and we have seen one answer: that at the cross we receive great pardon for terrible sin. But there is another answer. For the grace of

23 MacDonald, *Unspoken Sermons*, 74.

God serves as a bread-crumb trail, leading us up from the forgiveness itself to the forgiver. That is, in the light of the cross, Christians not only thank God for his grace to us but also begin to praise him for how gracious he is, for how beautifully kind and merciful he reveals himself to be in the cross. "Oh! that a great God should be a good God," wrote John Bunyan, "a good God to an unworthy, to an undeserving, and to a people that continually do what they can to provoke the eyes of his glory; this should make us tremble."[24] Indeed, he explained elsewhere:

> There is nothing in heaven or earth that can so awe the heart, as the grace of God. 'Tis that which makes a man fear, 'tis that which makes a man tremble, 'tis that which makes a man bow and bend, and break to pieces. Nothing has that majesty, and commanding greatness in and upon the hearts of the sons of men as has the grace of God.[25]

In his "Treatise on the Fear of God," Bunyan was insistent that the deepest and most powerful change of heart toward a true fear of God comes at the foot of the cross, where our sin and God's judgment and grace are supremely revealed. With striking wisdom, Bunyan wrote of how the cross simultaneously cancels the believer's guilt *and* increases our appreciation of just how vile our sinfulness is:

> For if God shall come to you indeed, and visit you with the forgiveness of sins, that visit removeth the guilt, but increaseth the sense of thy filth, and the sense of this that God hath forgiven a filthy

24 John Bunyan, "The Saints' Knowledge of Christ's Love," in *The Works of John Bunyan*, ed. George Offer, 3 vols. (Glasgow: W. G. Blackie & Son, 1854; repr., Edinburgh: Banner of Truth, 1991), 2:14.

25 John Bunyan, "The Water of Life," in *The Works of John Bunyan*, 3:546–47.

sinner, will make thee both rejoice and tremble. O, the blessed confusion that will then cover thy face.[26]

It is a "blessed confusion," made of sweet tears, in which God's grace and kindness shown to you at the cross make you weep at your wickedness. You simultaneously repent and rejoice. His mercy accentuates your wickedness, and your very wickedness accentuates his grace, leading you to a deeper and more fearfully happy adoration of the Savior.

And, to be clear, it is not just that we marvel at the forgiveness itself. Left there we could still be full of self-love, not *enjoying* the Savior but *using* him hypocritically as the one who'll get us out of hell free. The heart change that happens at the cross leads us *away* from ourselves to wonder at the Savior's gracious capacity for such forgiveness. We are led from the gift to wondering at the glory of the giver, from marveling at what he has done for us to marveling at who he is in himself. His magnanimity and utter goodness undo us and fill us with a fearful and amazed adoration. Said Spurgeon:

> *God's goodness often fills us with amazement*, and amazement has in it an element of fear. We are astonished at the Lord's gracious dealings with us, and we say to him, "Why hast thou been so good to me, for so many years, and in such multitudes of forms? Why hast thou manifested so much mercy and tenderness toward me? Thou hast treated me as if I had never grieved or offended thee. . . . O God, thy love is like the sun; I cannot gaze upon it, its brightness would blind my eyes! I fear, because of thy goodness."[27]

26 John Bunyan, "A Treatise on the Fear of God," in *The Works of John Bunyan*, 1:440.
27 Spurgeon, "A Fear to Be Desired," 499, his emphasis.

We Need Fearful, Fear-Inducing Preaching

If the fear of God is "the whole duty of man" (Eccles. 12:13), "the soul of godliness," and the essence of the new heart, then every believer should regularly pray with David,

Teach me your way, O LORD,
   that I may walk in your truth;
   unite my heart to fear your name. (Ps. 86:11)

Every believer should daily read Scripture and seek out books and fellowship that will be cross-centered and God-glorifying so that he or she might grow in this delighted fear.

But the importance of the fear of God puts a particular challenge to all those called to feed Christ's people with the word of God. First, if the people are ever to fear God aright, with wonder and not with dread, they need leaders who have that right fear and who model it in how they live and how they talk every day. Fear is a state of the heart, but one we have seen in Scripture that often manifests itself physically. In other words, fear will out. The presence or absence of fear in a leader should, to some extent, be sensed by the people. It should be something—perhaps unnamable but beautifully Christlike—in the atmosphere around him. He should be clearly *affected* by the beauty and glory and majesty and goodness of God.

Second, the fear of God should be a key goal of all our teaching. And that must shape both the *content* and the *intent* of our teaching. As for content, the people need the word of God if they are to grow in this fear. They need an expository, Scripture-rich diet. Through the Scriptures they need to be given the knowledge of God the Creator, but also brought beyond that to a cross-centered knowledge of God the Redeemer in Christ. They need to know the doctrine of justification by Christ's blood alone to banish their sinful fears, and to have the glory of the crucified one constantly placarded before them so that they grow in a wondering, filial fear.

As for the *intent* of our ministry, we must, like Moses, teach with the specific aim *that the people might fear the Lord* (Deut. 6:1–2). This means that the knowledge of God we seek to instill is, as Calvin put it, "not that knowledge which, content with that empty speculation, merely flits in the brain, but that which will be sound and fruitful if we duly perceive it, and if it takes root in the heart."[28] In other words, we cannot be content simply to transmit information as we teach. There is no true knowledge of God where there is no true fear of God. Pure and real religion is precisely where faith is "joined with an earnest fear of God."[29] Why? For the living God is so tremendously glorious in all his ways that he cannot be known without being adored. "How," Calvin asked, "can the mind be aroused to taste the divine goodness without at the same time being wholly kindled to love God in return? For truly, that abundant sweetness which God has stored up for those who fear him cannot be known without at the same time powerfully moving us."[30]

For the preacher, this means that a sermon cannot be confused with a simple lecture. Christian preaching is not merely explaining the text. The Pharisees could do that (with a theological correctness that exceeded the Sadduccees), and still they remained spiritually barren. The preacher has a greater responsibility (a responsibility that demands a deeper integrity): God shares knowledge of himself in order that we might be *affected*. Just as all theology should be

28 Calvin, *Institutes*, 1.5.9.
29 Calvin, *Institutes*, 1.2.2.
30 Calvin, *Institutes*, 3.2.41.

doxological, so all preaching should foster sincere worship. And such heartfelt, God-fearing worship is precisely what is most essentially and practically transformative for the Christian, what is most productive of true obedience. That is because love for God enables true love for neighbor (1 John 4:7–21). The first table of the law (concerning worship) is the foundation for the second (concerning love for neighbor), and only in that order can the law be fulfilled.[31]

This was something that clearly exercised Jonathan Edwards, living in a day when most people would have had a theoretical knowledge of at least some Christian basics. Such knowledge, he was clear, did not make them Christian; devils have that kind of knowledge. Instead, he argued, "True religion, in great part, consists in holy affections."[32] By this he meant that the true convert is palpably moved beyond indifference: "The motion of the blood and animal spirits begins to be sensibly altered" to love for Christ and joy in him.[33] Edwards rightly mentions love and joy, but given what we have seen of fear as the intense *sort* of love and joy Christians are to have, he could as well have said "fear." In fact, the biblical theme of the fear of God accentuates Edwards's argument. Our love for Christ and joy in him are meant to be not lukewarm but pulse-raising and blood-moving.

This, wrote Edwards, is why God has ordained preachers:

And the impressing divine things on the hearts and affections of men, is evidently one great and main end for which God has ordained, that his Word delivered in the holy Scriptures, should be opened, applied, and set home upon men, in preaching. And

---

31 Calvin, *Institutes*, 2.8.11.

32 Jonathan Edwards, *Religious Affections*, ed. John E. Smith, vol. 2 of *The Works of Jonathan Edwards* (New Haven, CT: Yale University Press, 1959), 95.

33 Edwards, *Religious Affections*, 96.

therefore it do[es]n't answer the aim which God had in this institution, merely for men to have good commentaries and exposi-
tions on the Scripture, and other good books of divinity; because,
although these may tend, as well as preaching, to give men a good
doctrinal or speculative understanding of the things of the Word
of God, yet they have not an equal tendency to impress them on
men's hearts and affections. God hath appointed a particular and
lively application of his Word, to men, in the preaching of it, as
a fit means to affect sinners, with the importance of the things of
religion, and their own misery, and necessity of a remedy, and the
glory and sufficiency of a remedy provided; and to stir up the pure
minds of the saints, and quicken their affections, by often bringing the great things of religion to their remembrance, and setting
them before them in their proper colors, though they know them,
and have been fully instructed in them already (II Peter 1:12–13).
And particularly, to promote those two affections in them, which
are spoken of in the text, love and joy.[34]

As Edwards saw it, preaching is *more* than exposition; it involves
"lively application" and the intent to "quicken affections" by setting
the things of the gospel before the people "in their proper colors."
None of which should be confused with emotionalism or emotional
manipulation. Edwards helpfully distinguished between (1) our pass-
ing, superficial passions, which come and go with blood sugar levels,
and (2) affections, which are deep matters of the very grain of the
heart and its inclinations. He was not advocating whipping up the
crowds; he wanted preachers to do far more weighty work: to aim
the gospel at the basic desires and deepest loves of the human heart.

---

34 Edwards, *Religious Affections*, 115–16.

And how? Especially by presenting the cross, for the

glory and beauty of the blessed Jehovah, which is most worthy in itself, to be the object of our admiration and love, is there exhibited in the most affecting manner that can be conceived of, as it appears shining in all its luster, in the face of an incarnate, infinitely loving, meek, compassionate, dying Redeemer. . . . So has God disposed things, in the affair of our redemption, and in his glorious dispensations, revealed to us in the gospel, as though everything were purposely contrived in such a manner, as to have the greatest, possible tendency to reach our hearts in the most tender part, and move our affections most sensibly and strongly. How great cause have we therefore to be humbled to the dust, that we are no more affected![35]

If indeed the fear of God is so essential a matter for Christian health, we who are called to preach cannot preach in such a way that allows for indifference. As we have seen, the word of God is described as being itself "the fear of the LORD" (Ps. 19:9): it cannot go out listlessly. It cannot be rightly received coolly or unaffectedly. We preachers must share the fiery *intent* of that word, preaching so that sinners tremble and that the hearts of saints no longer creep in dread but quake in wonder.

35 Edwards, *Religious Affections*, 123–24.

7

The Awesome Church

NOW IS A GOOD TIME to put down this book and ask yourself what things you fear. Our fears are highly revealing. What you fear shows what you really love. We fear our children getting hurt because we love them. We fear losing our jobs because we love the security and identity they give us. We fear rejection and criticism because we love approval. Some of these fears are healthy, some are overblown, and some betray deeper sicknesses in our character. Some we would hardly even label as fears at all. That fear of the leak in the roof, the fear that I left the oven on: they are more like background niggles, anxieties so petty they seem insignificant. Yet they are telling.

So ask yourself: What do my fears say about me and my priorities, about what I treasure? What do they say about where I am looking for security?

Which do you fear more: being sinful or being uncomfortable? God or man? *Being* a sinner or being *exposed* before others as a sinner?

Our fears are like ECG readings, constantly telling us about the state of our hearts.

So, what does it look like when a believer is filled with a right, healthy, filial fear of God? Not a cold, dead, outward, hypocritical *show* of reverential religion, but a heartfelt quaking at the goodness and greatness and glory of the Redeemer.

Deeper Communion with God

Scripture is jam-packed with promises of the many benefits enjoyed by those who fear God rightly. "Blessed is the man who fears the Lord," says Psalm 112:1. Why? Because "anyone who fears him and does what is right is acceptable to him" (Acts 10:35). Such a person is greatly loved by God.

> For as high as the heavens are above the earth,
> so great is his steadfast love toward those who fear him.
> (Ps. 103:11)

Indeed,

> As a father shows compassion to his children,
> so the Lord shows compassion to those who fear him.
> (Ps. 103:13; see also Judg. 10:16; Isa. 63:9)

Moreover,

> The Lord takes *pleasure* in those who fear him,
> in those who hope in his steadfast love. (Ps. 147:11)

Therefore, the "fear of the Lord is a fountain of life" (Prov. 14:27), for the Lord is a shield to them (Pss. 33:20; 34:7; 115:11); he fulfills their desire, "hears their cry and saves them" (Ps. 145:19), and lavishes goodness on them (Ps. 31:19). John Bunyan summarized this beautifully when he wrote:

> Child of God, thou that fearest God, here is mercy nigh thee, mercy enough, everlasting mercy upon thee. This is long-lived

mercy. It will live longer than thy sin, it will live longer than temptation, it will live longer than thy sorrows, it will live longer than thy persecutors. It is mercy from everlasting to contrive thy salvation, and mercy to everlasting to weather it out with all thy adversaries. Now what can hell and death do to him that hath this mercy of God upon him? And this hath the man that feareth the Lord.[1]

Those who fear the Lord know his mercy, love, and compassion. They can know they are accepted, protected, and delighted in. The fear of the Lord, then, is a heart-level indicator of the warm communion with God that God wants with his children. It is the wondering temperament of those who have been brought to know and enjoy the everlasting mercy of God and who therefore take pleasure in the one who takes pleasure in them. It is the mark of those who are being brought into the joy and life of Christ their Savior and who therefore share his delight in the fear of the Lord. Believers who have a right fear of the Lord, who know God and know these promises, will bemoan their prayerlessness but will know something of a heartfelt, affectionate prayer life. They will want to know God better and enjoy sweeter and more constant communion with him.

Knowledge and Wisdom

"The fear of the LORD is the beginning of knowledge," wrote Solomon (Prov. 1:7), for the fear of the Lord gives believers a knowledge no natural-born genius ever has.

---

1 John Bunyan, "A Treatise on the Fear of God," in *The Works of John Bunyan*, ed. George Offer, 3 vols. (Glasgow: W. G. Blackie & Son, 1854; repr., Edinburgh: Banner of Truth, 1991), 1:470.

Since Adam and Eve ate from the tree of the knowledge of good and evil, mankind has chased a particular sort of knowledge: knowledge without God. But the more we have pursued that knowledge, the more filled with fears we have become. We tremble at the terrifying size of the universe and despair at the dark complexity of the human psyche. Without God, more knowledge has not meant more happiness and satisfaction; it has left modern man feeling adrift on a vast sea of fears. At the same time, all that long quest for knowledge has left us profoundly ignorant: ignorant of the Maker and so the very logic of reality, and ignorant of who we are and who we were made to be. Wrote Calvin:

> The greatest geniuses are blinder than moles! Certainly I do not deny that one can read competent and apt statements about God here and there in the philosophers, but these always show a certain giddy imagination. As was stated above, the Lord indeed gave them a slight taste of his divinity that they might not hide their impiety under a cloak of ignorance. And sometimes he impelled them to make certain utterances by the confession of which they would themselves be corrected. But they saw things in such a way that their seeing did not direct them to the truth, much less enable them to attain it! They are like a traveler passing through a field at night who in a momentary lightning flash sees far and wide, but the sight vanishes so swiftly that he is plunged again into the darkness of the night before he can take even a step—let alone be directed on his way by its help. Besides, although they may chance to sprinkle their books with droplets of truth, how many monstrous lies defile them! In short, they never even sensed that assurance of God's benevolence toward us (without which man's understanding can only be filled

with boundless confusion). Human reason, therefore, neither approaches, nor strives toward, nor even takes a straight aim at, this truth: to understand who the true God is or what sort of God he wishes to be toward us.[2]

In contrast, the fear of the Lord brings a knowledge beyond the grasp of any of those great philosophers. For the fear of the Lord is precisely that "assurance of God's benevolence toward us." In the fear of the Lord is found a true knowledge of God, as Creator and as Redeemer, as majestic and as merciful. Any "knowledge of God" that is devoid of such fearful and overwhelmed wonder is actually blind and barren. The living God is so wonderful that he is not truly known where he is not worshiped and heartily adored.

There is a particular challenge here for those of us who love theology. All too easily our theological studies can become exercises in puffing ourselves up and lording it over others. Thus Helmut Thielicke warned his theological students of the vain stage of "theological puberty" many go through after a year or two of study.[3] In that stage, infatuated with new theological concepts, the young theologian is filled with a gnostic pride. His love dies in the devilish thrill of acquiring a knowledge that means power. Then this skewed knowledge proves its own perversity in his character as he becomes a graceless theological thug, ever itching for a chance to show off his prowess. And it is hardly as if older theologians are immune to this disease. We who love theology need to remember that there is no true knowledge of God where there is no right fear of him. The fear

2 John Calvin, *Institutes of the Christian Religion*, ed. John T. McNeill, trans. Ford Lewis Battles (Louisville: Westminster John Knox, 2011), 2.2.18.

3 Helmut Thielicke, *A Little Exercise for Young Theologians* (Grand Rapids, MI: Eerdmans, 1996), 15.

of God is the only possible foundation upon which true knowledge is built: all knowledge acquired elsewhere is counterfeit and will eventually prove itself as such.

But the fear of the Lord is not only the beginning of knowledge *of God*. It is also the beginning of true knowledge of ourselves. Early in his *Institutes*, Calvin wrote that "man is never sufficiently touched and affected by the awareness of his lowly state until he has compared himself with God's majesty."[4] Only in the light of God's holiness and majesty do I truly understand how puny, how vicious, and how pathetic I naturally am. In other words, I do not have a true knowledge of myself if I do not fear God. Without that fear, my self-perception will be wildly distorted by my pride and by the messages of the sinful culture around me. It is when we are most thrilled with God and his redemption that our masks slip and we see ourselves for what we really are: creatures, sinners, forgiven, adopted.

The fear of the Lord is also—and is most famous for being—the beginning of wisdom (Prov. 9:10). Sharing Christ's own God-fearing perspective, and sharing the same Spirit of knowledge, wisdom, and fear (Isa. 11:2), believers grow in a Christlike wisdom as they grow in this fear. The insight and knowledge they have been given—about God, themselves, and the world—enables them to walk through life wisely. And so, with the word of God serving as a map to reality, the fear of God is a compass to steer believers aright.

Now, truth be told, the fear of God is a very unexpected compass and guide to wisdom. When we look for wisdom, we instinctively look to our own *intelligence* or the superior intelligence of others. We struggle to distinguish between intelligence and wisdom. Which is

4 Calvin, *Institutes*, 1.1.3.

odd, given how the world is littered with clever fools—people with high IQs and a history of quite stupid life choices. As a few minutes in most science labs or academic meetings will tell you, mere intelligence is not a safe guide to walking through life wisely. We need the fear of God to steer our abilities, and without it, all our abilities are a liability. Take the brilliant young theological thug online: he may just be as bright as he thinks he is, but his untempered ability only makes him more dangerous.

And therein lies a challenge for those conscious of their own ability, and a comfort for all who feel daunted by the talents of others. It is only this wonderful fear of God that can steer us wisely through life. This—not IQ—is the beginning of wisdom. Therefore, says Psalm 115:13,

> He will bless those who fear the LORD,
>   *both the small and the great.*

For it is not talent that God blesses so much as the fear of God.

The fear of the Lord makes believers both knowledgeable and wise. In fact, in essential matters—in knowing God, ourselves, and the nature and story of the universe—the fear of the Lord makes believers more knowledgeable than the greatest geniuses, and wiser than the wisest sages.

Becoming like God

The knowledge of God that the fear of the Lord brings is not a sterile knowledge. Those who fear God come to know him in such a way that they actually become holy, faithful, loving, and merciful, like him. Abraham's faithfulness to God in offering his son Isaac, for example, is proof that he feared God (Gen. 22:12). For, like a fire in the heart, the fear of the Lord has a purifying effect: "By the fear of the LORD one turns away from evil" (Prov. 16:6; see also Ex. 20:20). It consumes sinful desires and fuels holy ones. And the word "desires" there is key, for the fear of the Lord does not keep believers from sin in the sense that it makes us merely alter our behavior for fear of punishment. Rather, it brings us to *adore* God and so loathe sin and long to be truly and thoroughly like him.

Becoming like God must mean becoming happy. God, after all, is "the blessed" or happy God (1 Tim. 1:11). The Spirit we are given is the Spirit of the fear of the Lord, who causes us to share Christ's *delight* in the fear of the Lord (Isa. 11:2–3). To fear God is to enter that blessed divine life. You naturally expect that the fear of God would make you morose and stuffy, but quite the opposite. Unlike our sinful fears, which make us twitchy and gloomy, the fear of God has a profoundly uplifting effect: it makes us happy. How can it not when it brings us to know this God? Notice, for example, how "the fear of the Lord" and "the comfort of the Holy Spirit" are paired in the early church's experience: "So the church throughout all Judea and Galilee and Samaria had peace and was being built up. And walking *in the fear of the Lord and in the comfort of the Holy Spirit*, it multiplied" (Acts 9:31). For to fear God is to know the Spirit's consolation and Christ's own happiness and satisfaction in God.

Along with making us happy, the fear of the Lord makes believers large-hearted, like God. Think of the lovely little story of the prophet Obadiah, in the days of Elijah:

> Now the famine was severe in Samaria. And Ahab called Obadiah, who was over the household. (Now Obadiah feared the LORD greatly, and when Jezebel cut off the prophets of the LORD, Obadiah took a hundred prophets and hid them by fifties in a cave and fed them with bread and water.) (1 Kings 18:2–4)

Far from making Obadiah self-involved and frosty, the fear of God made him profoundly generous and compassionate to those hunted prophets in need. For the fear of the Lord is the precise opposite of hard-heartedness. Indeed, Proverbs 28:14 deliberately contrasts the two:

> Blessed is the one who fears the LORD always,
> but whoever hardens his heart will fall into calamity.

That softheartedness and large-heartedness toward others is actually the overflow of a prior love: our tenderheartedness and affection toward God. It means that those who fear God have—to use another much-misunderstood word—a jealousy for God. Charles Spurgeon explained:

> It is one of the most solemn truths in the Bible, "The Lord thy God is a jealous God." We might have guessed it, for great love has always that dangerous neighbour jealousy not far off. They that love not have no hate, no jealousy, but where there is an intense, an infinite love, like that which glows in the bosom of God, there must be jealousy.[5]

Such righteous jealousy should not be confused with selfish envy: it is a love that will not let go of the beloved or make do with substitutes. As God the Father is jealous for his beloved Son, and as Christ is jealous for his bride, the church, so too those who fear God find in themselves a loving jealousy for God. They become jealous in the same way that he is jealous. Adoring him, they cannot abide his glory being diminished or stolen by idols or by people. False teaching will distress them, not because it contradicts their views but because it

---

5 C. H. Spurgeon, "Godly Fear and Its Goodly Consequence," in *The Metropolitan Tabernacle Pulpit Sermons*, 63 vols. (London: Passmore & Alabaster, 1855–1917), 22:233.

impugns *him*. Self-righteousness becomes loathsome to them because of how it steals from the glory of his grace.

Then, from this sensitive appreciation of God in all his glory grows another Christlike quality: humility. "So do not become proud, but fear," wrote Paul (Rom. 11:20), for trembling in wonder at God keeps one from trusting in oneself. It is the key to true humility, which is not about trying to think less of yourself or trying to think of yourself less but about marveling more at him. A true and happy fear of God simply eclipses self. It is, in other words, *the* antidote to pride and the prayerlessness that springs from pride. When God is so marvelous in our eyes that we rejoice and tremble, we cannot but praise him and throw ourselves on him in hearty and dependent prayer. We cannot be great in our own eyes or self-dependent. Not only that, but this fear levels and unites us as a church. In light of God's merciful magnificence, we find ourselves leveled before him as mere creatures and sinners. This fear admits no boasting before God and so admits no elite and no second-class in the church. And because this fear is such a loving adoration, it also binds together all who are leveled before God. Fear gathers us together in the warm and humble fellowship of a shared love.

Joyful, loving, humble, and jealous for God, the right fear of God makes the difference between hollow, devilish religiosity and beautiful, Christlike believers. It also makes the difference between hollow, grasping, professionalized ministries and life-giving ministries of delighted and satisfied integrity.

Finding Strength

In *The Holy War*, his allegorical story of the siege of the town of Mansoul, John Bunyan introduces his readers to Mr. Godly-fear, a man of "courage, conduct and valour."[6] Mr. Godly-fear embodied Bunyan's conviction that the fear of the Lord gives believers strength, especially in the face of anxieties and the fear of man. John Flavel agreed and wrote that the "carnal person fears man, not God; the strong Christian fears God, not man; the weak Christian fears man too much, and God too little."[7]

We don't tend to talk much about "the fear of man" today: we call it people-pleasing, peer pressure, or codependency. Some classic signs of it are the overcommitment that comes from an inability to say no, self-esteem issues, and an excessive sensitivity to the comments, views, and behavior of others. And need I even mention our fear of evangelism?

Codependency is seen as such a problem today that it has spawned a whole therapeutic industry and made millions for airport pop-psychology books. Western culture has come to view low self-esteem as the root of our every emotional problem, holding us back in life. The normal prescription for building your self-worth on the opinion of others is to love yourself more; love yourself so much that it will hardly matter what others think. In other words, treat the disease of narcissism with more narcissism. It's hardly surprising: we're living downstream from the early nineteenth-century philosopher Hegel, of whom it has been said, "Hegel's only real fault was that he confused himself with the last judge; but that is quite a fault."[8] But what clearly is surprising for the culture is that the cure doesn't work. Seeking to bolster our self-esteem by making us *more* self-referential and *more* self-conscious is only making us more vulnerable and thin-skinned.

6   John Bunyan, "The Holy War," in *The Works of John Bunyan*, 3:351.
7   John Flavel, "A Practical Treatise on Fear," in *The Whole Works of John Flavel*, vol. 3 (London: W. Baynes and Son, 1820), 241.
8   Robert W. Jenson, *The Knowledge of Things Hoped For: The Sense of Theological Discourse* (Oxford: Oxford University Press, 1969), 233.

According to Scripture, that turn inward on ourselves is precisely our problem, not the solution. Indeed, it is the very heartbeat of sin, as Martin Luther famously put it when he argued that Scripture "describes man as so *turned in on himself* that he uses not only physical but even spiritual goods for his own purposes and in all things seeks only himself."[9] More self-love, self-confidence, or trust in man will never ease our fears: relief from anxious fears is for those who fear and trust the Lord.

> Thus says the LORD:
> "Cursed is the man who trusts in man
>   and makes flesh his strength,
>   whose heart turns away from the LORD.
> He is like a shrub in the desert,
>   and shall not see any good come.
> He shall dwell in the parched places of the wilderness,
>   in an uninhabited salt land.
>
> "Blessed is the man who trusts in the LORD,
>   whose trust is the LORD.
> He is like a tree planted by water,
>   that sends out its roots by the stream,
> and does not fear when heat comes,
>   for its leaves remain green,
> and is not anxious in the year of drought,
>   for it does not cease to bear fruit." (Jer. 17:5–8)

Luther's own experience, in facing dreadful odds, was that the fear of the Lord was his medicine overcoming his other fears. At

---

9 Martin Luther, *Luther's Works*, vol. 25, *Lectures on Romans*, ed. Jaroslav Jan Pelikan, Hilton C. Oswald, and Helmut T. Lehmann (St. Louis, MO: Concordia, 1999), 345.

the Diet of Worms in 1521, the night before he had to face the emperor and an expected death sentence, his friends urged him "to be brave, to act manfully, and not to fear those who can kill the body but cannot kill the soul, but rather revere Him who is able to cast both soul and body into hell [Matt. 10:28]."[10] The next day, he would famously declare: "I am bound by the Scriptures I have quoted and my conscience is captive to the Word of God. I cannot and I will not retract anything."[11] Immediately before that, though, he explained to the emperor his motivation: "We ought to think how marvelous and terrible is our God in his counsels, lest by chance what is attempted for settling strife grows rather into an intolerable deluge of evils, if we begin by condemning the Word of God. . . . Therefore we must fear God."[12]

This also seems to have been the very lesson the apostle Peter learned. Clearly, Peter struggled with fear of men, betraying Christ three times the night before the crucifixion, and then later betraying the gospel in Antioch through "fearing the circumcision party" (Gal. 2:12). The readers of his first letter would presumably have known all that. And so with characteristic self-humbling, he shared the wisdom he himself had learned: "Even if you should suffer for righteousness' sake, you will be blessed. Have no fear of them, nor be troubled, but in your hearts honor Christ the Lord" (1 Pet. 3:14–15).

So *how* can the fear of the Lord free us from our anxieties and our fear of man? Essentially, it acts like Aaron's staff, which ate up the staffs of the Egyptian magicians. As the fear of the Lord

10 Martin Luther, *Luther's Works*, vol. 32, *Career of the Reformer II*, 108.
11 *Luther's Works*, 32:112.
12 *Luther's Works*, 32:111–12.

grows, it outgrows, eclipses, consumes, and destroys all rival fears. So the Lord could advise Isaiah: "Do not call conspiracy all that this people calls conspiracy, and *do not fear what they fear*, nor be in dread. But the LORD of hosts, him you shall honor as holy. *Let him be your fear*, and let him be your dread" (Isa. 8:12–13). When the fear of the Lord becomes central and most important, other fears subside. Likewise, Joshua would urge the Israelites before entering Canaan: "Do not fear the people of the land, for they are bread for us. Their protection is removed from them, and the LORD is with us; do not fear them" (Num. 14:9). And Jesus offers very similar counsel in the Sermon on the Mount. In telling his disciples not to worry, he gets them to look away from their worries to the kingdom of God:

> Therefore do not be anxious, saying, "What shall we eat?" or "What shall we drink?" or "What shall we wear?" For the Gentiles seek after all these things, and your heavenly Father knows that you need them all. But seek first the kingdom of God and his righteousness, and all these things will be added to you. (Matt. 6:31–33)

In this, Jesus is not merely distracting his disciples from their worries, like a parent waving a toy when a toddler cries. He is reorienting their perspective. For our fears act like a blinding, disorienting fog, stopping us from seeing anything else. So Jesus puts God and his kingdom as the sun in the sky of their perspective, both *above* everything and *enlightening* everything.

To be clear, the fear of the Lord does not eclipse and consume other fears simply because it sees God is bigger than the other things I fear, though there certainly is that. The delighted fear of the merciful Redeemer helps here, just as much as the awed fear of the Creator. It is beauty that kills the raging beast of anxiety. See, for example, how in Psalm 27 David speaks of the Lord's "light" and "salvation" as the balm for his fears. When describing the Lord as his stronghold, refuge, and joy, David focuses on the *beauty* of the Lord:

> The LORD is my light and my salvation;
> > whom shall I fear?
> The LORD is the stronghold of my life;
> > of whom shall I be afraid?
>
> When evildoers assail me
> > to eat up my flesh,
> my adversaries and foes,
> > it is they who stumble and fall.
>
> Though an army encamp against me,
> > my heart shall not fear;
> though war arise against me,
> > yet I will be confident.
>
> One thing have I asked of the LORD,
> > that will I seek after:
> that I may dwell in the house of the LORD
> > all the days of my life,
> to gaze upon the beauty of the LORD
> > and to inquire in his temple.
>
> For he will hide me in his shelter
> > in the day of trouble;
> he will conceal me under the cover of his tent;
> > he will lift me high upon a rock.
>
> And now my head shall be lifted up
> > above my enemies all around me,

and I will offer in his tent
   sacrifices with shouts of joy;
I will sing and make melody to the LORD. (vv. 1–6)

Here is truth for every Christian who needs the strength to rise above his or her anxieties, or who needs the strength to pursue an unpopular but righteous course. The fear of the Lord is the only fear that *imparts* strength. This is an especially vital truth for any who are called to some form of leadership, for the strength this fear gives is—uniquely—a *humble* strength. Those who fear God are simultaneously humbled *and* strengthened before his beauty and magnificence. Thus they are kept gentle and preserved from being overbearing in their strength. (Significantly, Peter pairs "gentleness" with "fear" ["respect," φόβος (*phobos*)] in 1 Pet. 3:15.) The fear of the Lord is, then, the medicine for what Luther saw as the two main faults of pastors:

> But let us call these two faults by name: softness and harshness. Concerning the former, Zech. 11:17 says: "O shepherd and idol, you who desert the flock." Concerning the latter, Ezek. 34:4 says: "With force and harshness you have ruled them." These are the two main faults from which all the mistakes of pastors come.[13]

Pastors or not, all of us are temperamentally inclined to lean one way or another. Some are natural rhinos: strong and thick-skinned, but not gentle. Others are more like deer: sweet and gentle, to be sure, but nervous and flighty. The fear of the Lord corrects and beautifies both temperaments, giving believers a gentle strength. It makes them—like Christ—simultaneously lamblike and lionlike.

13 *Luther's Works*, 25:139.

Church history testifies to how the fear of God can mold such believers. Both John Calvin and Charles Spurgeon, for example, confessed their natural inclination to be timid and fearful. Yet, as they grew in the fear of God, they became gentle and lamblike lions in the cause of the gospel. It is clear that Spurgeon was teaching a lesson he himself had learned when he shared with his congregation this story of the English Reformer Hugh Latimer:

> It was bravely done by old Hugh Latimer when he preached before Harry the Eighth. It was the custom of the Court preacher to present the king with something on his birthday, and Latimer presented Henry VIII with a pocket-handkerchief with this text in the corner, "Whoremongers and adulterers God will judge"; a very suitable text for bluff Harry. And then he preached a sermon before his most gracious majesty against sins of lust, and he delivered himself with tremendous force, not forgetting or abridging the personal application. And the king said that next time Latimer preached—the next Sunday—he should apologise, and he would make him so mould his sermon as to eat his own words. Latimer thanked the king for letting him off so easily. When the next Sunday came, he stood up in the pulpit and said: "Hugh Latimer, thou art this day to preach before the high and mighty prince Henry, King of Great Britain and France. If thou sayest one single word that displeases his Majesty he will take thy head off; therefore, mind what thou art at." But then said he, "Hugh Latimer, thou art this day to preach before the Lord God Almighty, who is able to cast both body and soul into hell, and so tell the king the truth outright." And so he did. His performance was equal to his resolution. However, the king did not take off his head, he respected him all the more. The fear of

the Lord gave him strong confidence, as it will any who cleave close to their colours.

> "Fear him, ye saints, and ye will then
> Have nothing else to fear."[14]

The Battle of Fears in the Christian Life

Since fear is a matter of the heart, reorienting our fears is no easy, quick matter. And we have an enemy whose spiteful aim is to make us afraid of God and afraid of everything, who would have us sulk and tremble. But reorienting our fears and affections is a daily battle we must join, as both a duty and a joy.

William Bates explains why it is a duty:

> Consider, as the throne endures no rivals, so that fear which is a homage and tribute which we should pay only to the Sovereign Creator of the world, should not be given to the creature. He that doth immoderately fear the creature, dethrones God and deifies man. It is no less than sacrilege to alienate the affections from God; and it is no less than idolatry, to place our affections inordinately upon the creature.[15]

We were made to place this most intense affection upon God, and we are out of kilter with reality if we set it elsewhere. Thus, when this adoring homage is paid to anyone or anything else, God is robbed of his right and we are robbed of our happiness. But Bates goes on (in starkly uncomfortable words) to argue that this misplacing of our fears has a terrifying trajectory:

---

14 Spurgeon, "Godly Fear and Its Goodly Consequence," 237.
15 William Bates, "On the Fear of God," in *The Whole Works of the Rev. W. Bates*, vol. 3 (London: James Black, 1815), 223.

Consider, this immoderate fear of the creature is the root of apostacy. Such a man will rather save his life than his soul, such a person carries his faith about him at the mercy of every one that threatens to kill him: for this is a maxim, he that is a coward will be an apostate. That man doth not fear God, that dares not die for him; that man that hath not got above the love of life, and above the fear of death, will never be a martyr, he will never hold out for God; therefore such a person is in the very next degree to an apostate.[16]

Bates has set out two different paths: the road to heaven, which is a path of growth in an adoring, filial fear of God; and the road to hell, which is a downhill path of snowballing anxieties and terrors. This means that our sinful fears cannot be nursed or left to fester: we must fight fear with fear.

But that fight is not only a duty but also a joy. Left to our sinful fears of God, we will shrink from God in guilt and not enjoy all his goodness. Left to our fear of man, we will wilt before every criticism, unable to enjoy real fellowship. Which is just what our enemy will encourage. And just as a right and happy fear of God is fostered by the truth, sinful fears grow in a bed of Satan's lies. Said Bunyan:

Satan is always for being too soon or too late. If he would have men believe they are children, he would have them believe it while they are slaves, slaves to him and their lusts. If he would have them believe they are slaves, it is when they are sons, and have received the spirit of adoption, and the testimony, by that, of their sonship before. And this evil is rooted even in his nature; "He is a liar, and

16 Bates, "On the Fear of God," 223.

the Father of it"; and his lies are not known to saints, more than in this, than he labours always to contradict the work and order of the Spirit of truth [John 8].[17]

Satan's lies would rob believers of their filial fear and leave them with a groveling dread of God and a competitiveness instead of any real fellowship between us. We must counter with the truth that drives out anxiety. Into the battlefield of our troubled hearts we send the promises of God. For the word that brings a right fear of God (Ps. 19:7–9) brings freedom (James 1:25). Safe in Christ, we testify to ourselves afresh that the Almighty is our compassionate Redeemer and loving Father, and that he is able, willing, and near to us as we call on him. We remember:

> The LORD is righteous in all his ways
>   and kind in all his works.
> The LORD is near to all who call on him,
>   to all who call on him in truth.
> He fulfills the desire of those who fear him;
>   he also hears their cry and saves them. (Ps. 145:17–19)

In the face of our culture of anxiety, having this right fear of God will beautifully adorn and attest to the reality of the gospel we proclaim. For thereby we can give the lie to the atheist claim that liberating ourselves from the fear of God will make a less fearful culture. Quite the opposite: we can show that this fear—which is pleasurable and not disagreeable—is precisely what can liberate us from the anxieties now flooding our increasingly post-Christian Western culture.

---

17 Bunyan, "A Treatise on the Fear of God," 453.

Sharing God's Fearsomeness

Song of Songs ("Song of Solomon," ESV) has a beautiful insight for us here. Jonathan Edwards argued that the very title "Song of Songs" sets for us a high expectation of its content:

> The name by which Solomon calls this song confirms me in it that it is more than an ordinary love song, and that it was designed for a divine song, and of divine authority; for we read, 1 Kings 4:32, that Solomon's "songs were a thousand and five." This he calls the "song of songs" [Canticles 1:1], that is, the most excellent of all his songs, which it seems very probable to me to be upon that account, because it was a song of the most excellent subject, treating of the love, union, and communion between Christ and his spouse, of which marriage and conjugal love was but a shadow.[18]

Song of Songs has two main characters: the lover and his beloved. The lover is a shepherd-king, like David (1:4, 7); but he is the Son of David (3:7). He stands at the door and knocks in 5:2–3. His carriage in chapter 3 looks like the tabernacle/temple; and like the Lord in the exodus, he comes up from the wilderness like a pillar of smoke (v. 6), all perfumed with the scents of the temple. The beloved is described as being like Israel in the exodus, coming up from the wilderness leaning on her lover (8:5). Like Israel in Isaiah 5:1–7, she is repeatedly compared to a vineyard, and to Jerusalem (Song 8:10–12). And while she is his bride, she is also his sister (4:9): Christ is the church's bridegroom and brother, but, given the taboo on marrying one's sister in Leviticus

---

18 Jonathan Edwards, *Notes on Scripture*, ed. Stephen J. Stein, vol. 15 of *Works of Jonathan Edwards* (New Haven, CT: Yale University Press, 1998), 92n147.

18:9, it seems highly unlikely that this could describe an ordinary Jewish romance.[19]

Ordinary lovers are parted by death, but the love of these lovers is as strong as death. Not even floodwaters can wash it away (Song 8:6–7). It all looks as if Song of Songs is primarily describing that unique story of the love between Christ and the church. And the overall similarity of the book to Psalm 45, which the New Testament cites as referring to Christ, is striking. It is no wonder, then, that Song of Songs, like Revelation, ends with the bride calling, "Come!"

Within that context, the bridegroom makes a statement about the bride that is eye-catching:

> You are beautiful as Tirzah, my love,
>> lovely as Jerusalem,
>> awesome as an army with banners. . . .
>
> "Who is this who looks down like the dawn,
>> beautiful as the moon, bright as the sun,
>> awesome as an army with banners?" (Song 6:4, 10)

The bride is like an army. And she is bright like the sun, with the reflected beauty of the moon. From the shy and embarrassed girl we met in 1:5–7, she has become *awesome*. As Moses's face reflected the glory of the Lord, the church comes to reflect the bridegroom's awesome magnificence. We know from the apostle Paul that, by the Spirit, believers are being transformed into the image of Christ "from one degree of glory to another" (2 Cor. 3:18). But what we read here

---

19 This paragraph and the next draw from my foreword to Richard Sibbes, *The Love of Christ: Expository Sermons on the Verses from Song of Solomon Chapters 4–6*, Puritan Paperbacks (Edinburgh: Banner of Truth, 2011).

in Song of Songs specifies that this transformation is a growth in *reflected awesomeness.*

Led by the Spirit into conformity with Christ, the church begins to exhibit to the world fearsome divine qualities of holiness, blessedness, happiness, wholeness, and beauty. Thus the church shines like the moon in the darkness, eliciting both wonder and dread. Believers become like heaven's Solid People in Lewis's *The Great Divorce*: their very wholeness and loving joyfulness are fearful to others. This combination is deeply alluring and inexplicable, yet at the same time troubling to unbelievers for how it exposes their grumbling crookedness. In the fear of God, believers become—like their God—blessedly and beautifully fearsome.

8

Eternal Ecstasy

IN THE PRESENCE OF THE LORD, everyone trembles. Before him, Abraham, Joshua, David, Ezekiel, Daniel, Paul, and John all fell on their faces (Gen. 17:3; Josh. 5:14; 1 Chron. 21:16; Ezek. 1:28; Dan. 8:17; Acts 9:4; Rev. 1:17). Overcome by the tremendousness of his glory, people are so overwhelmed, they think they will die (Judg. 13:20–22). But it is not just people who tremble. In Isaiah's vision of the Lord enthroned in the temple, "the foundations of the thresholds shook at the voice of him who called" (Isa. 6:4). And it doesn't stop there: at his appearing,

> the mountains quake before him;
>> the hills melt;
> the earth heaves before him,
>> the world and all who dwell in it. (Nah. 1:5)

For he is the one "who looks on the earth and it trembles" (Ps. 104:32).

It should be no surprise, then, that all things will shake and tremble at the second coming of Christ. At Sinai "his voice shook the earth, but now he has promised, 'Yet once more I will shake not only the earth but also the heavens'" (Heb. 12:26). But what sort of trembling is this that will grip the universe? For the heavens and the earth, it is clearly a trembling of exultation. Thus, when David brought the ark/throne of God to Jerusalem, he sang of the day that event prefigured:

> Tremble before him, all the earth;
>   yes, the world is established; it shall never be moved.
> Let the heavens be glad, and let the earth rejoice,
>   and let them say among the nations, "The LORD reigns!"
> Let the sea roar, and all that fills it;
>   let the field exult, and everything in it!
> Then shall the trees of the forest sing for joy
>   before the LORD, for he comes to judge the earth.
> Oh give thanks to the LORD, for he is good;
>   for his steadfast love endures forever! (1 Chron. 16:30–34;
>   see also Ps. 96:11–13)

The earth shakes with pleasure, for it is joining in with the joy of believers as their filial fear swells with delight at the presence of their God.

> For the creation waits with eager longing for the revealing of the sons of God. For the creation was subjected to futility, not willingly, but because of him who subjected it, in hope that the creation itself will be set free from its bondage to corruption and obtain the freedom of the glory of the children of God. For we know that the whole creation has been groaning together in the pains of childbirth until now. (Rom. 8:19–22)

At one time, "the glory of the LORD filled the LORD's house," and when all the people of Israel saw "the glory of the LORD on the temple, they bowed down with their faces to the ground on the pavement and worshiped and gave thanks to the LORD, saying, 'For he is good, for his steadfast love endures forever'" (2 Chron. 7:1–3). But on that last day, the glory of the Lord will fill the whole earth, and his people will fall down in fearsome wonder, delight, and praise.

Yet, at the same time, at the same appearance of the Lord in glory, the sinful fear of unbelievers will swell into a horrified dread as they hide "themselves in the caves and among the rocks of the mountains, calling to the mountains and rocks, 'Fall on us and hide us from the face of him who is seated on the throne, and from the wrath of the Lamb, for the great day of their wrath has come, and who can stand?'" (Rev. 6:15–17). Where the final appearing of the Lord in glory fills believers with an unprecedented joyful fear of the Redeemer, it fills unbelievers with a new level of dread at their Judge.

That day will usher in a new age in which both the sinful fears of unbelievers and the right fear of believers will crescendo. Both sorts of fear will climax and become eternal states—an ecstasy of terror, on the one hand, and delight, on the other.

Hell Is a World of Fear

Hell—the destiny of all unbelievers—will be a dreadful place. Death is "the king of terrors" (Job 18:14), and hell will be the place of eternal death. It will be the ultimate sump of all sinful fears, heaving with a shared dread of holiness. There, like the demons who believe and shudder (James 2:19), its occupants will hate God and the exposing light of his glory. Before him there, "Every heart will melt, and all hands will be feeble; every spirit will faint, and all knees will be weak as water" (Ezek. 21:7). Just as the kings of the earth will call to the mountains and rocks "hide us from the face of him who is seated on the throne" (Rev. 6:16), so in hell they will long to hide. "It is a fearful thing to fall into the hands of the living God" (Heb. 10:31), and all in hell will have done so, but without ever turning to him. They will be like the terrified sinners in Zion described by Isaiah:

> Trembling has seized the godless:
> "Who among us can dwell with the consuming fire?
> Who among us can dwell with everlasting burnings?"
> (Isa. 33:14)

Sin first made the world a place full of fear, and hell is its culmination: a place of unrelieved fears, and of sinful fear come to a head.

Heaven Is a World of Fear

In 1738, Jonathan Edwards preached a series of sermons on 1 Corinthians 13, a series he concluded with the observation, "Heaven is a world of love."[1] He could as well have said that heaven is a world of fear, for the love he described there is a fearfully ecstatic joy and wonder. Saints there, he said, will be "like a flame of fire with love."[2] Where hell is the dreadful sewer of all sinful fears, heaven is the paradise of unconfined, maximal, delighted *filial* fear.

Right now, heaven is the home of this happy fear. "The pillars of heaven tremble" (Job 26:11). Why? For it is the dwelling place of "the Fear,"

---

1 Jonathan Edwards, "Charity and Its Fruits," in *Ethical Writings*, ed. Paul Ramsay, vol. 8 of *The Works of Jonathan Edwards* (New Haven, CT: Yale University Press, 1989), 366–97.
2 Edwards, "Charity and Its Fruits," 379.

a God greatly to be feared in the council of the holy ones,
   and awesome above all who are around him. (Ps. 89:7)

There the "holy ones" delight to fear him, for they see him clearly.
They tremble before him as the Creator:

You rule the raging of the sea;
   when its waves rise, you still them.
You crushed Rahab like a carcass;
   you scattered your enemies with your mighty arm.
The heavens are yours; the earth also is yours;
   the world and all that is in it, you have founded them.
   (Ps. 89:9–11)

But the "holy ones" also look deeper into his holiness to see the
character behind his creative omnipotence. They delight in him as
the loving Redeemer:

Righteousness and justice are the foundation of your throne;
   steadfast love and faithfulness go before you.
Blessed are the people who know the festal shout,
   who walk, O LORD, in the light of your face,
who exult in your name all the day
   and in your righteousness are exalted.
For you are the glory of their strength;
   by your favor our horn is exalted.
For our shield belongs to the LORD,
   our king to the Holy One of Israel. (Ps. 89:14–18)

In heaven they cry,

Worthy are you, our Lord and God,
   to receive glory and honor and power,

for you created all things,
    and by your will they existed and were created. (Rev. 4:11)

And they cry,

Worthy is the Lamb who was slain,
    to receive power and wealth and wisdom and might
    and honor and glory and blessing! (Rev. 5:12)

And who are these adoring inhabitants of heaven? Primarily, angels (though saints join in their praise). Now, it is worth taking a moment to look at the angels' fear-filled worship of God, for they model in heaven how God is to be worshiped. In heaven, angels are called to worship God (Heb. 1:6), and they do so eagerly and fervently, falling on their faces before the throne (Rev. 4:10; 7:11; 11:16). In Isaiah 6, the seraphim fly above the throne of the Lord crying,

Holy, holy, holy is the LORD of hosts;
    the whole earth is full of his glory! (v. 3)

With two wings they cover their faces, presumably to shield them from the overwhelming sight of God's unveiled glory. The word "seraph" derives from the Hebrew verb שָׂרַף (*sarap*, "burn"), suggesting that they burn with a holy love, the flame of the Lord (Song 8:6). This heavenly host delights in the God in whose presence there is fullness of joy (Ps. 16:11), and they delight in his mighty acts. At the birth of Christ, they burst forth in praise, singing,

Glory to God in the highest,
    and on earth peace among those with whom he is pleased!
    (Luke 2:14)

At the creation,

> the morning stars sang together
> and all the sons of God shouted for joy. (Job 38:7)

That last verse is just one example of the strong connection in Scripture between stars and angels, and it actually reinforces how the angels (or "sons of God") model to us a right, filial fear. We see the connection in John's vision in Revelation, where "the seven stars are the angels of the seven churches" (Rev. 1:20). But think, too, of the divine title "the LORD of hosts [or "armies"]." Sometimes it is clear that those "hosts" are angelic armies (1 Kings 22:19; Ps. 148:2); sometimes they are clearly stars (Deut. 4:19; 17:3; 2 Kings 23:5; Ps. 33:6); and sometimes all distinction is broken down, as when

> from heaven the stars fought,
> from their courses they fought against Sisera. (Judg. 5:20)

Aware of this connection, Jonathan Edwards commented on Genesis 15:5 (where Abraham is promised that his offspring will be like the stars): "The stars were designed by the creator to be a type of the saints, the spiritual seed of Abraham. And the seeming multitude of them, which is much greater than the real multitude of visible stars, was designed as a type of the multitude of the saints."[3] As the Lord fills the universe with countless stars, so he will fill his creation with the sons of God. And like the angelic "sons of God," the saints will shine "like the stars forever and ever" (Dan. 12:3). They will be "like angels in heaven" (Matt. 22:30) as they gather there around

---

3   Jonathan Edwards, *The "Blank Bible,"* ed. Stephen J. Stein, vol. 24 of *The Works of Jonathan Edwards* (New Haven, CT: Yale University Press, 2006), 157.

the throne. As the radiant angels now fall on their faces in fearful, ecstatic joy and adoration before God, so one day will all the saints.

Nothing Else to Fear

Because we tend today to think of fear as a wholly negative thing, it jars us to think of fear remaining in heaven, or of fear being part of our eternal blessedness. But the fear of the Lord endures forever (Ps. 19:9), such that voices in heaven can cry, "Fear God and give him glory" (Rev. 14:7), and

> Who will not fear, O Lord,
>   and glorify your name? (Rev. 15:4)

and

> Praise our God,
>   all you his servants,
> you who fear him,
>   small and great. (Rev. 19:5)

To be sure, in heaven there will no longer be anything of which to be *afraid*. There the children of God will finally be out of the reach of all danger. We will be purified and behold God clearly, and so our fears will be rightly aligned: there will be no fear of punishment, nor any trace of any sinful fear of God left in us. We will rejoice to know him as he is, with no distortion, no misunderstanding, and no devilish whispers of doubt.

Instead, our clear apprehension of God will then enhance our wondering, trembling adoration. And then, when we are resurrected, our resurrection bodies will be "spiritual bodies" so that we might fully bear the image of the man of heaven (1 Cor. 15:44, 49). Filled with the Spirit of the fear of the Lord, we will share Christ's own delight in the fear of the Lord (Isa. 11:2–3). Not afraid of anything, the saints will be caught up into God's own fearful happiness and will be overwhelmed by exultation in the glory of God. In other words, our eternal joy will consist precisely in this fear of God: rejoicing and marveling so entirely that, like the angels, we burn and tremble and fall on our faces in wonder. Jonathan Edwards put it this way:

> As they increase in the knowledge of God and of the works of God, the more they will see of his excellency; and the more they see of his excellency, *cæteris paribus* ["all other things being equal"], the more will they love him; and the more they love God, the more delight and happiness, *cæteris paribus*, will they have in him.[4]

Moreover, beholding him, we will become like him. For now, "we all, with unveiled face, beholding the glory of the Lord, are being transformed into the same image from one degree of glory to another. For this comes from the Lord who is the Spirit" (2 Cor. 3:18). But then "we shall be like him, because we shall see him as he is" (1 John 3:2). Made entirely Christlike at last, we ourselves shall become fearfully glorious beings, sharing his fearsome beauty. John Bunyan captured something of this in the second part of *The Pilgrim's Progress* where the pilgrims are clothed with fine, white linen:

> When the women were thus adorned, they seemed to be a terror one to the other; for that they could not see that glory each one

---

4 Jonathan Edwards, *The "Miscellanies," Entry Nos. a–z, aa–zz, 1–500*, ed. Thomas A. Schafer, vol. 13 of *The Works of Jonathan Edwards* (New Haven, CT: Yale University Press, 1994), 275–76.

had in herself, which they could see in each other. Now therefore they began to esteem each other better than themselves. For, You are fairer than I am, said one; and, You are more comely than I am, said another. The children also stood amazed, to see into what fashion they were brought.[5]

Without any fake self-abasement, we shall be self-forgetfully radiant and, at the same time, glorious and entranced only with that glory outside ourselves. Beautiful as the moon, bright as the sun, the saints will be awesome as an army with banners.

Like Flames of Fire

In the last couple of centuries, Christians have known that talk of heaven sounds faintly ridiculous in secularized and materialistic cultures. They have therefore tended to be more measured than their forebears when speaking of it, focusing on the basic need to establish its scriptural truthfulness. It is striking, then, to compare modern treatments of heaven with those of older generations, who were far more ready to speak of heavenly raptures and the emotional intensity of our heavenly experience. Those earlier generations wanted to impress on believers that to be in the presence of God will give us not a tepid happiness but a quaking, fearfully overwhelmed, ecstatic pleasure.

The hymnwriter Isaac Watts is an example:

In heaven the blessed inhabitants behold the majesty and greatness of God in such a light as fixes their thoughts in glorious wonder and the humblest adoration, and exalts them to the highest pleasure and

---

5 John Bunyan, "The Pilgrim's Progress: From This World to That Which Is to Come," in *The Works of John Bunyan*, ed. George Offer, 3 vols. (Glasgow: W. G. Blackie & Son, 1854; repr., Edinburgh, Banner of Truth, 1991), 3:190.

praise. . . . When lips are not only directed to speak this sublime language, but the soul, as it were, beholds God in these heights of transcendent majesty, it is overwhelmed with blessed wonder and surprising delight, even when it adores in most profound holiness and self-abasement. This is the emblem of the worship of the heavenly world.[6]

And Watts again:

And, O my thinking powers, are ye not sweetly lost in this holy rapture, and overpowered with divine pleasure, O my soul, in such meditation as this? Art thou not delightfully surprised with the thoughts of such self-sufficiency and such an inconceivable perfection? . . . I both rejoice and tremble.[7]

Or here is Edwards:

If we can learn anything of the state of heaven from the Scripture, the love and joy that the saints have there, is exceeding great and vigorous; impressing the heart with the strongest and most lively sensation, of inexpressible sweetness, mightily moving, animating, and engaging them, making them like to a flame of fire.[8]

For, as F. W. Faber put it so lyrically:

And Father! when to us in heaven
Thou shalt Thy Face unveil,
Then more than ever will our souls
Before Thy goodness quail.

6 Isaac Watts, *The World to Come* (London: W. Baynes, 1817), 271–72.
7 Watts, *The World to Come*, 278–80.
8 Jonathan Edwards, *Religious Affections*, ed. John E. Smith, vol. 2 of *The Works of Jonathan Edwards* (New Haven, CT: Yale University Press, 1959), 114.

Our blessedness will be to bear
The sight of Thee so near,
And thus eternal love will be
But the ecstasy of fear.[9]

We get an appetizer of this heavenly and perfected filial fear in this life when we sing heartily in worship together.

> Shout to God with loud songs of joy!
> For the LORD, the Most High, is to be feared. (Ps. 47:1–2)

We catch its scent when the gospel, the Scriptures, or even some beauty in creation makes us well up or drop to our knees in sweet adoration. That overwhelmed sense when our bodies react unbidden to the strength of our affection is a small preview of the day when we will fall at our Lord's feet, too full of joy to stand.

In fact, all fears are a foretaste. The sinful fears and dreads of unbelievers are the firstfruits of hell; the filial fears of Christians are the firstfruits of heaven. Now our fears are partial; then they will be unconfined. For now, Christians see in part, and so we love and rejoice only in part. We hang our heads knowing that moments of filial, trembling wonder are all too faint and all too few. But when we see him as he is, that ecstasy will be unimpaired and absolute. Using touching pastoral compassion, Edwards once compared the poverty of our current spiritual experience with the perfection of heaven. In this world, he explained, Christians are hindered in their worship and delight in God.

> They have a great deal of dullness and heaviness. They carry about with them a heavy moulded body, a lump of flesh and blood which

---

9 F. W. Faber, "The Fear of God," in *Faber's Hymns* (New York: Thomas Y. Crowell & Co., 1894), 101.

is not fitted to be an organ for a soul inflamed with high exercises of divine love, but is found a great clog to the soul, so that they cannot express their love to God as they would. They cannot be so active and lively in it as they desire. Fain would they fly, but they are held down, as with a dead weight at their feet. Fain would they be active as a flame of fire, but they find themselves, as it were, hampered or chained down, that they cannot do as their love inclines them. Love disposes them to praise, but their tongues are not obedient; they want words to express the ardor of their souls, and cannot order their speech by reason of darkness, Job 37:19. And oftentimes for want of expressions they are forced to content themselves with groans that cannot be uttered, Romans 8:26. But in heaven they shall have no such hindrance. They will have no dullness or unwieldiness, no corruption of heart to fight against divine love and hinder suitable expressions, no clog of a heavy lump of clay, or an unfit organ for an inward heavenly flame. They shall have no difficulty in expressing all their love. Their souls, which are like a flame of fire with love, shall not be like a fire pent up but shall be perfectly at liberty.[10]

Edwards was describing the quantum difference between our cloddish current state and the vigor and totality of our spiritual liveliness in heaven. Yet, even now the Spirit is enlivening believers. From the moment of regeneration, when he breathes new life into a soul, the Spirit's work is to move us from spiritual lethargy to vivaciousness, where we share Christ's own vitality and delight in the fear of his Father. And that work is precisely all about growth in the fear of the Lord. To fear the Lord is to be more *alive*; it is for our love, joy,

10 Edwards, "Charity and Its Fruits," 378–79.

wonder, and worship of God to be more acute and affecting. For when we rejoice in God so intensely that we quake and tremble, then are we being most heavenly.

The Expulsive Power of a Filial Fear

Perhaps the most famous sermon ever delivered in the historic pulpit of the Tron Church in Glasgow was Thomas Chalmers's "The Expulsive Power of a New Affection." In it he argued that nobody can "dispossess the heart of an old affection, but by the expulsive power of a new one."[11] His point was that we cannot simply will ourselves to love God more; the love of sin can be expelled only by the love of God. Chalmers could have been speaking of fear, for the filial fear of God is the soul of godliness and the essence of the new life implanted by the Spirit. It is the ultimate affection and the very aroma of heaven. It is the affection that expels our sinful fears and our anxieties. It is the affection that expels spiritual lethargy. To grow in this sweet and quaking wonder at God is to taste heaven now.

---

11 Thomas Chalmers, "The Expulsive Power of a New Affection," in *Posthumous Works of the Rev. Thomas Chalmers*, vol. 6 (New York: Harper & Brothers, 1848–1850), 253.

General Index

Scripture Index

Union

We fuel reformation in churches and lives.

Union Publishing invests in the next generation of leaders
with theology that gives them a taste for a deeper knowledge
of God. From books to our free online content, we are
committed to producing excellent resources that will refresh,
transform, and grow believers and their churches.

We want people everywhere to know, love, and enjoy God,
glorifying him in everything they do. For this reason, we've
collected hundreds of free articles, podcasts, book chapters,
and video content for our free online collection. We also
produce a fresh stream of written, audio, and video resources
to help you to be more fully alive in the truth, goodness, and
beauty of Jesus.

If you are hungry for reformational resources that will help
you delight in God and grow in Christ, we'd love for you to
visit us at unionpublishing.org.

unionpublishing.org

Also Available
from Michael Reeves

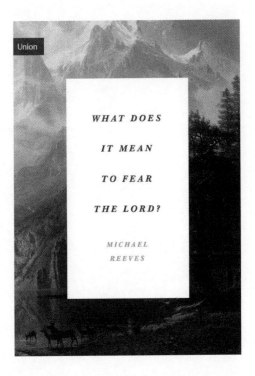

Michael Reeves calls us to see God as the object of our fear—a fear marked not by anxiety, but by the enjoyment of God. As we learn to truly fear the Lord, we will take part in the pivotal role the church plays in exhibiting his divine qualities of holiness, blessedness, happiness, wholeness, and beauty to the world.

For more information, visit **crossway.org**.